THE DIVINE MADMAN
The Sublime Life and Songs
of Drukpa Kunley

THE DIVINE MADMAN
The Sublime Life and Songs of Drukpa Kunley

Translated by
KEITH DOWMAN AND SONAM PALJOR

Illustrated by
LEE BAARSLAG

PILGRIMS

PILGRIMS PUBLISHING
Varanasi ♦ Kathmandu

The Divine Madman
Keith Dowman

Published by:
PILGRIMS PUBLISHING

An imprint of:
PILGRIMS BOOK HOUSE
(Distributors in India)
B 27/98 A-8, Nawabganj Road
Durga Kund, Varanasi-221010, India
Tel: 91-542-2314060,
Fax: 91-542-2312456
E-mail: pilgrims@satyam.net.in
Website: www.pilgrimsbooks.com

First published by The Dawn Horse Press,
Clearlake, California.
Reprinted with permission.
Copyright © 2000, Pilgrims Publishing
All Rights Reserved

ISBN: 81-7769-013-2

Printed in India at Pilgrim Press Pvt. Ltd. Lalpur Varanasi

Namo Buddhaya

This translation is dedicated to
Meryl and Ariane

CONTENTS

Editor's Introduction

Drukpa Kunley and the Crazy Wisdom Method of Teaching

by Georg Feuerstein

This volume records some of the stories about the Adept Drukpa Kunley (Tib.: 'Brug-pa Kun-legs), which to this day are favorites of the people of Tibet and the surrounding regions. Whatever the historical credibility of these stories may be, they deserve our full attention for two reasons: first, because Drukpa Kunley counts among the most celebrated Adepts of the Himalayan countries, and second, because he belonged to the tradition of "Crazy Wisdom," of which precious little is known in the West.

Like that other great and in the West better known Tibetan Adept Milarepa (1040–1123), Drukpa Kunley was a "madman" (*smyon-pa*), an Enlightened "eccentric." But unlike Milarepa, who was a celibate teaching by means of poetry and song, Drukpa Kunley used poetry, song, dance, humor, drink, and not least sex to Teach his contemporaries the great Lesson of spiritual life: that the individual being, with its countless likes and dislikes, is constantly immersed in the universal Reality-Bliss beyond all personal preferences, feelings, and thoughts; that the phenomenal world (*samsara*) is indeed coessential with the transcendental Reality (*nirvana*).

Drukpa Kunley, in the style of all the "divine madmen" before and after him, was a relentless critic of what the modern Crazy Adept Da Free John calls the "usual man"—whether he has donned a monk's garb or labors in the field. Drukpa Kunley mocked the secular and religious establishment, railed against commonplace morality and conventionalism, and lashed out against the narrow-mindedness of the earthling who does little more than stake out and defend his own insular existence.

The Spiritual Master is indeed a voice that rises in this wilderness, to Awaken every neighbor from the illusion of his acre of land, his ordinary pond, his body-mind. It is a necessary voice, the voice that sounds whenever the Truth of human experience is Revealed to one who is Awake. Therefore, such a one speaks, even with urgency and anger. It is the prophetic voice, the awful shout, expressed with all the gestures of frustrated Divinity.[1]

The motivation for Drukpa Kunley's unusual exploits was not personal gain or self-aggrandizement, but the spontaneous desire to Enlighten others. "What I do is not the way I am, but the way I teach"[2] is Master Da's explanation of the Crazy Adept's unorthodox Teaching methods. "Care-free renunciation, an excess of compassion, total lack of inhibition, skilful use of shock-therapy, tears and laughter, are the specific characteristics of the divine madman," writes the translator of this volume (p. 28).

In the West, but also in the East—wherever religious fundamentalism or a dualistic metaphysics holds reign, spiritual life is characteristically viewed in opposition to material, bodily existence. If it is regarded as legitimate at all, as it barely is in our society, it is generally promoted as an other-worldly, ascetical, and ethereal pursuit. Such spirituality is based on the presumption that Man is a disembodied, unfeeling, sexless, and relationless entity.

Crazy Wisdom Adepts have an altogether different view of Man and life in general. For them, Enlightenment is a whole-bodily Realization that does not presuppose a world-negative attitude, a disposition of mystical inversion, and esoteric ascent of awareness. They know Reality to be here and now and nondistinct from the creative struggle of life. As Master Da Free John writes:

> We must surrender to and into the Present God. God is not elsewhere in relation to us now. God is always Present, Alive as all beings, Manifest as the total world. Our obligation is not to invert and go elsewhere to God, nor to extrovert and exploit ourselves in the self-possessed or anti-ecstatic mood that presumes God to be absent or non-existent. Our obligation is to Awaken beyond our selves, beyond the phenomena of body and mind, into That in which body and mind inhere. When we are thus Awakened, our lives become

1. Bubba [Da] Free John, *The Enlightenment of the Whole Body* (Middletown, Calif.: The Dawn Horse Press, 1978), p. 152.

2. Ibid., p. 53.

the Incarnation Ritual of Man, whereby only God is evident and only God is the Process of the present and the future. That Way of Life is not bound to this world or any other world, nor to any form of attention in body or mind. Rather, the Way of Life is Ecstatic, God-Made, Free, Radiant, and always already Happy.[3]

Although Drukpa Kunley, being a Buddhist, did not use the term "God," the mood of his Teaching is nevertheless akin to that of Master Da. By his own testimony always "relaxing in the stream of events" (p. 93) and "never working, letting reality hang loosely" (p. 133), Drukpa was continually and spontaneously communicating the great Truth of "Emptiness"—that "whatever arises is the Path of Release" (p. 133). This is what Master Da calls seventh-stage Wisdom.

One who abides in the Self of God in the seventh stage of life is Awake to God under all conditions. He inheres in God through Self-Realization (the moment to moment re-cognition of attention) and, as the Self, inheres in God as Infinite Radiant Bliss. The Self is Awake to the Radiance of God. All objects, all arising conditions are found to be a transparent Play on the Radiant Immensity of the Divine Person. Thus, in the seventh stage of life, the soul inheres in God as the Self, and the Self inheres in God through re-cognition of everything in God.

Therefore, in the seventh stage of life, the soul is Awake as Love, or Ecstatic Worship of the Transcendental and All-Pervading Divine Person. All inwardness is transcended. All obsession with experiences, objects, and others is transcended. There is constant re-cognition of all arising conditions of experience, but all the while there is natural abiding in the Ecstatic Love of God through radical intuition of the Condition of everything.

Thus, in the seventh stage of life, the arising of attention and experience is not at all prevented. The soul Awakens from its exile in the world and its seclusion in the heart.

3. Da Free John, *Scientific Proof of the Existence of God Will Soon Be Announced by the White House!* (Middletown, Calif.: The Dawn Horse Press, 1980), p. 312.

There is only Ecstasy, or Perfect God-Love. Attention has been Transformed, so that it is simply the Radiance of the Self, rather than the binding gesture of an independent consciousness.[4]

From the Realizer's aerial view of existence, the world process is essentially chaotic, nonsensical, and utterly undependable. Where the conventional, ego-entrenched mind anxiously clings to meanings of its own making, and thereby exposes itself to repeated frustration and suffering, the Enlightened being sees the non-binding nature of all arising conditions—and encounters them with a sense of irrepressible humor. Perceiving God or Reality equally in everything, he neither shies away from anything nor becomes obsessed with any experience or idea. Because he is radically and irrevocably Free, he can also abstain from them without repressing any latent desires or tendencies. For the Realizer, life is Divine Creativity or Play (*lila*). In the language of Sufism, he is "drunk with God," which sacred inebriation makes him immune to the "poison of the world."

In his God-intoxication or Ecstasy, however, he is prone to behave at odds with the all-too-sober world of social convention. In the eyes of the world, therefore, he is a radical, an anarchist or eccentric—a lunatic. His very existence calls into question the established order. Living, as he does, out of the plenitude of the Whole, he has no need for any self-limitation. His entire life is a towering symbol, a constant demonstration, of the fact that the limitations the "usual man" presumes are merely neurotic strategies to introduce a semblance of stability and orderliness into the incessant flux of events that constitutes phenomenal existence.

The "divine madman" demonstrates that it is not necessary to sleep eight hours a day to feel good, or to eat three meals a day to maintain the body in a fit condition, or to abstain from sexual intercourse to promote spiritual growth. By his anomalous and erratic behavior he spotlights the absurdity of all fixed, man-made rules and prescriptions, whether they are designed to

4. Bubba [Da] Free John, *The Enlightenment of the Whole Body*, p. 527.

regulate mundane activities or spiritual life. His very unusualness serves as a mirror to evince the intrinsic lopsidedness of conventional experiencing, thinking, feeling, and doing. He is an iconoclast who is wont to smash all our carefully erected conventional images of the world. In the light of his sublime Realization, our ideas about life, our pet theories, and our venerable customs are all seen to be merely huge prisons built on sand.

Conventional religiosity and spirituality are not exempted from the Crazy Adept's criticism and ridicule. Nothing is sacred to him who moves in, and is moved by, the Sacred itself. Whatever springs from the human mind or heart can never be more than an effigy—a fragile image of the Real. And the God-Realized Adept, who is at one with the Real, will not suffer substitutes. He has emerged from the dark cave with its phantom shadows, and his whole life acts as a reminder that mankind's true place is in the Divine Light.

In India such a great being is also known as an *avadhuta*. The esoteric significance of this word is explained in the *Kularnava-Tantra* (chapter X) as follows:

> *a* = the Immutable (*akshara*)
> *va* = the Excellent (*varenya*)
> *dhu* = shaken off (*dhuta*) the fetters of the world
> *ta* = "That Thou art" (*tat tvam asi*)

Thus, each syllable is a pointer to the transcendental Realization of the *avadhuta*. This is how the *Siddha-Siddhanta-Paddhati* (chapter VI), one of the earliest Hathayoga texts, describes the Crazy Adept:

> He who is firmly stationed in the center of the world, devoid of all [fearful] trembling, whose freedom-from-dejection [serves as] his loin cloth and *kharpara*-stone—he is styled an *avadhuta* (v. 5).

> Whose limit is [naught but] the Supreme Consciousness, whose knowledge of the [Ultimate] Object [serves as] his sandals, and whose great vow [serves as] his antelope skin—he is styled an *avadhuta* (v. 7).

> Whose Light of Consciousness and Supreme Bliss [serve as] his pair of earrings, who has ceased recitation with a rosary—he is styled an *avadhuta* (v. 9).

Who moves with his inner-being into the Unthinkable,
into the remote Region within, who has that very Place
as his undergarment—he is styled an *avadhuta* (v. 12).

Who always turns round fully into the very center of
himself and who views the world with equanimity—he is
styled an *avadhuta* (v. 15).

Who is firmly established in his own Luminosity, who is
the Lustre of the nature of the Bright, who delights in
the world through Play—he is styled an *avadhuta*
(v. 19).

Who is sometimes an enjoyer, sometimes a renouncer,
sometimes a nudist or like a demon, sometimes a king,
and sometimes well-behaved—he is styled an *avadhuta*
(v. 20).[5]

The last stanza makes direct reference to his protean nature.
He is a trickster who can turn himself into anything at all. He
assumes no fixed roles and statuses. One day, or perhaps one
minute, he will act the beggar, and the next moment he will
behave like an emperor. Thus, Hari Giri Baba (twentieth
century), of Vaijapur in Aurangabad district, India, was well
known for occasionally dressing up like a king. He would wear
silk and brocade, expensive shoes, and a stately turban and
expect to be treated like royalty. And then again he would go
about naked like the poorest beggar.

Understandably, discipleship under such a God-Realized
Adept is a hard school, but conceivably also the most direct
way to Realization. For, the student will have to abandon all
ideas of predictability and emotional security. His only assurance
is that the Adept will do his utmost to serve his Awakening. The
devotee's principal task is to recognize in his Teacher an Agent
of the Enlightenment Process and simply surrender to him as
such. Master Da Free John observes:

> Many so-called spiritual seekers are just Narcissus[6] in
> drag. They don't have enough gut for spiritual life. They are

5. Editor's translation.

6. Narcissus, the self-lover of Greek mythology, is a key symbol in
Master Da Free John's description of Man as a self-possessed seeker,
enamored with what he does not recognize as his own image, one who

not interested in the demand that is the *Guru*. They are dogs coming for a bone. . . . [The dog] does whatever he must, until his master gives him the bone. And then he runs away with the bone. . . . He doesn't go back to his master again until he's out of bone. He does not go to his master in order to be with him, to delight in him, to be mastered by him. He only goes for another bone. Such is the ordinary spiritual seeker. . . . But the Master waits for his true disciple to come and submit to him.[7]

The disciple or devotee must come to understand that there is absolutely nothing to hold on to. In his surrender to the Adept, he has to learn perfect self-reliance, or rather, Self-reliance. Until then he will be tested again and again. For, it is only when one is totally immersed in the Bliss of the Whole that one realizes, moment to moment, the non-binding nature of all arising phenomena.

When the famous Buddhist scholar-saint Naropa approached his teacher-to-be, Tilopa, for instruction, the latter took him to a place where they met a prince in a chariot. Tilopa suggested that if he had a disciple, that disciple would drag the nobleman out of his chariot and manhandle him. Naropa, who had complete trust in the Wisdom of his newfound teacher, unhesitatingly followed this indirect command. He almost lost his life in the process because he was swiftly overpowered by the prince's bodyguard. Tilopa healed his wounds and then instructed him that "the deer of the body which believes in an I" deserves to be killed. Other similarly dramatic and unconventional lessons followed. On one level, the story of Naropa's spiritual tests is an allegory, though Crazy Adepts have been

suffers in dilemma, contracted upon himself at every level of the being from all relations and from the condition of relationship itself. "He is the ancient one visible in the Greek 'myth,' who was the universally adored child of the gods, who rejected the loved-one and every form of love and relationship, who was finally condemned to the contemplation of his own image, until he suffered the fact of eternal separation and died in infinite solitude." (Da Free John, *The Knee of Listening*, rev. ed. [Middletown, Calif: The Dawn Horse Press, 1978], p. 26).

7. Bubba [Da] Free John, *The Method of the Siddhas*, rev. ed. (Middletown, Calif.: The Dawn Horse Press, 1978), p. 137.

known to resort to such highly unorthodox ways of making a particular Teaching point.

The symbolic incidents mentioned in Naropa's biography and the concrete historical "lessons" of living Adepts all demonstrate the same underlying principle: that of transcending one's habitual self-limitation and fixation upon a particular aspect of the Whole. We tend to identify with certain roles and ritualistically expect certain responses from our environment. Life is movement, but the ego in its constant anxiety to place and secure itself in this eternal flux creates borders, fences, and walls where there are none. The ego itself is an illusion of solidity and stability. Consequently, it is the main target of the Crazy Adept's attack.

There is a story about Neem Karoli Baba (?-1973), who one evening was squatting in the street. A delegation of self-important notables came along to pay their respects to him. He invited them to sit down with him right there and then. It was not until they had done so, with much reluctance, that he consented to get up and accompany them to his nearby hermitage.

Swami Samarth, also known as Akkalkot Maharaj (?-1878), used to live in the home of one of his disciples. He would cause much upset by his eccentric behavior, especially to the disciple's wife, who was only a reluctant devotee. The Swami would often touch and thereby "pollute" the food before an offering could be made to the Divine, or feed the cows the precious grain, or pour water into the hearth. On one occasion he even expelled his disciple's family when his pupil was out of town, and it took much pleading before the great Teacher changed his mind. All these wayward acts are undoubtedly profoundly significant. But in every instance there is a deliberate infringement of egoic expectations, a bursting of customary forms of self-limitation.

Most Westerners, having been educated to worship reason and rational order, may find it particularly difficult to understand Crazy Wisdom and the Teaching methods and behavior of Crazy Adepts. Yet, there is a little-known tradition of "divine madmen" even within Christianity—a predominant western religion. But, estranged as we are from the religious roots of our culture, we know nothing of the living wisdom of those who followed the "glad tidings" of Jesus of Nazareth at the margins of the conventional (or orthodox) religious ethos. We have long forgotten the exemplary lives of Symeon of Emesa, Thomas of Coelesyria, Andreas of Constantinople, Lucas of Ephesus—all canonized saints *and* "divine madmen" or "Fools for Christ's Sake." They were all living examples of the foolishness of which St. Paul spoke in his first epistle to the Corinthians (1:25; 3:18; 4:10).

St. Symeon (sixth century), for instance, was once to sell beans for an innkeeper, but to the chagrin of his employer, he distributed them free to the people. On one occasion he was beaten for throwing nuts at people praying in church. He used to relieve himself in public, and would often walk about naked, throw stones at passersby, crawl on his belly, and associate with harlots (though without having sexual intercourse with them). He also regularly drank wine in taverns and often provoked violence or was himself violent without apparent reason. He also happened to work miracles, and these were often flavored with humor. He was buried as any madman, but when shortly afterwards his coffin was reopened to grant him a decent burial, his corpse was not to be found.

St. Andreas (ca. 880–946) was a kindred "eccentric." He would drink water from puddles, sleep in dirt, gorge himself on wine, and, like St. Symeon, visit harlots.

That it was not only the Eastern Orthodox Church that spawned such Wise Fools is evident from the life of the great Western Church father, St. Francis of Assisi (1184–1226). He referred to himself and his pupils as "jesters of the Lord," who practiced "spiritual joy." Although he never followed the excesses of "obscenity" of the Fools for Christ's Sake in the Eastern branch of Christianity, he did make a point of transgressing certain rules for the clergy and laity. Thus, on one occasion he preached stark naked in church, provoking shock and mockery.

Juniper (?–1258), a disciple of St. Francis, used similarly unconventional means to awaken his flock. His greatest offense was the sacrilegious act of clipping off adornments from the altar to aid a poor woman.

Understandably, "solid" citizens are traumatized and outraged by such capriciousness. But why are they shocked and offended? They simply feel threatened. And they have good reason to feel threatened, because after all, their "all-is-well" universe is at stake. By inclination we are loath to reconsider the (shaky) premises upon which our lives are built. Basically, we are scared to look at life as it really is. We want everything to be harmonious, orderly, in place. Deep down we are all "home-makers." Yet, the common message to mankind from those who are "mad" in God—whether they belong to the Christian tradition or to one of the Eastern religions or cultures—is that the material realm is not our "home" and that we are merely trapping ourselves in an illusion of familiarity.

Man is truly homeless in this finite realm, so long as he identifies and is obsessed with a particular aspect, or location, of the world. As that great Islamic mystic and poet Jalal ad Din Rumi wrote in his *Discourses* (section 15):

> In man there is a passion, an agony, an itch, an importunity such that, though a hundred thousand worlds were his to own, yet he would not rest nor find repose . . . All these [worldly!] pleasures and pursuits are as a ladder. Inasmuch as the steps of the ladder are not a place wherein to dwell and abide but are for pressing on, happy is he who the quicker becomes vigilant and aware. Then the road becomes short for him, and he wastes not his life upon the steps of the ladder.[8]

Man's only Home is the omnipresent Transcendental Being or Reality. It is our true Identity. All else is a phantom, an illusion, a dream. And it is this dream which the Adepts seek to dispel.

> Everyone is enchanted with un-Reality, enchanted with the conventional appearance of every moment, and therefore we cannot merely talk to people and break that spell. They are not just thinking wrongly. They are altogether associated with this moment in such a fashion that they are incapable of being Awake to their actual Condition. In effect, then, you cannot merely talk to them, you must cut them in half with a big sword. You must blow their minds. You must shake

---

8. A. J. Arberry, *Discourses of Rūmī* (London: John Murray, 1975), p. 75.

them loose. You must wholly divert them. You must trick them. You must be wild to truly Enlighten people.

You can be a friendly professorial yogi or teacher and communicate views of things that are simple sacred views or philosophical views of Reality as a sacred Condition. You can point to Consciousness, you can point to Mind, you can give people yogic techniques for inverting their attention. All of that can be done in a very orderly, gentlemanly manner, but it will not break the spell. It will not Awaken people. At most, it may help them harmonize their lives somewhat. It may even help them realize a certain level of gnosis or knowledge about things as they seem, but it will not Enlighten them. It will not break the spell of un-Enlightenment.

That task requires another kind of work altogether. Breaking that spell requires the Mad Work, the Crazy Work, the Wild Work of the Adept.[9]

Those who happen to come in contact with a Crazy Adept enter a whirlwind whose unpredictable currents sweep away anything that does not bend to the Divine Force or Siddhi. Yet, while the puritan or "serious" seeker is astounded, shocked, offended, and outraged, the "divine madman" is happily immersed in the unsurpassable Bliss of the Transcendental Reality. He is lodged in—he *is*—the still eye of the hurricane. He has transcended all duality and has become the "Self of all beings." This paradoxical, totally Crazy condition is the true seat of his exuberance and humor. Master Da Free John writes about his own Realization and Teaching as follows:

I am here to make a mockery of the universe, to demonstrate that the universe is a laughing matter, so that you will transcend it. I am here to tell the ultimate jokes—all seven of them. There are seven eternal jokes, which are not revealed in words—they are not quips or one-liners, but whole pieces of existence, or stages of life. The seven stages of life are the seven original jokes. They too are the fool of God. When you transcend them by fulfilling them, then you are able to see

9.   From an unpublished talk by Da Free John, September 25, 1982.

the wonderment of God. When you have fulfilled the Teaching of Truth, then you get the joke of human existence. Living the stages of life, though a profound and necessary gesture, is ultimately foolishness. The seven stages are stages of laughter, each of which must, in its turn, become a great laugh to you. You must be able to feel total pleasure in the face of each stage of experience before you can go on to complete the next stage. In your present level of realization, however, you have not yet laughed at any of the stages of life. You are still burdened by them, still carrying them around, still being tested by them. You are not yet laughing at God's fool. You yourself will become God's fool as you incarnate and laugh at each of the stages of life. Even the seventh stage of life, you will see, is a colossal lot of foolishness. The only way to move through the seventh stage is to laugh your head off. The seventh stage of life must become a laughing matter, along with all the rest of your body and all its stages of growth. You must get the seventh joke, which is the body itself, the last laugh. That joke is eternal and its Humor is Infinite Bliss.[10]

10. Da Free John, *Scientific Proof of the Existence of God Will Soon be Announced by the White House!* pp. 377–78.

Illustrations

Foreword

by Choegyal Gyamtso Tulku

The *Naljorpa* Drukpa Kunley was an awakened Buddha, a Master of *Mahamudra* and *Dzokchen*. I am very happy that English readers now have the opportunity to read a full account of a Tibetan *Mahasiddha*'s life. The stories in this biography are not fiction or fable – the events described really happened. The lovely stories the Master left behind him are associated with existing landmarks, temples, and homes. Even since Tibet has been closed to us, the pilgrim can still find faith in the *Naljorpa*'s power spots, and see his belongings, in the eastern Himalayas. This biography is full of inspiration.

The biographies of Tibetan saints are written in three distinct styles. The 'external biography' gives us factual information about the saint's life: where he was born; his youth; how the change in his mind took place; how he renounced the eight worldly preoccupations (praise and blame, loss and gain, pleasure and pain and notoriety and fame); how he gained an understanding of karma; how he met his teacher and took refuge in the Lama; how he practised his moral precepts, study, and meditation, to gain both relative and absolute compassion; how through the maintenance of his SAMAYA vows and his accomplishment of the two stages of Tantric practice, he brought his body, speech, and mind to full enlightenment. The external stories embody his teachings to common disciples and beginners, and show the events of his life in terms of ordinary perception.

The 'internal biography' emphasizes the inner life, describing the universe in terms of meditation experience,

stages of realization, Deities, *Dakinis*, YIDAM, and Buddhas
and their Pure Lands. It describes spiritual evolution in
terms of veins, subtle energies, and the essential, elemental
body (*rtsa rlung thig-le*).

In this work the stories are written mostly in the style of
the 'secret biography'. Here the Lama's life is fully revealed
in terms of his perfect activity, and there is no distinction
made between external events and the inner life. The path of
development has ended, and with complete abandon, the
Master is seen fulfilling the highest goal. He works without
any discrimination, inhibition, or selfish motivation, to
give meaning to other people's lives. It is called 'secret'
because without having realized the Lama's state of mind,
we cannot understand it, and because traditionally such
literature is kept hidden away from people who are following a pure *Hinayana* discipline or the path of *Mahayana*
altruism. An uncensored account of the Lama's activity is
likely to raise all sorts of doubts and fears in the minds of
devotees. Also, it is secret, a mystery, because a Buddha's
existence resolves the paradoxes and dualities of being. The
way Drukpa Kunley acts makes us understand how the
Three Precepts of the Three Vehicles (*Hinayana, Mahayana
and Vajrayana*) can be combined without any contradiction.

We should understand that in his secret biography
Drukpa Kunley takes his consorts like Milarepa, who took
Tseringma to assist him in the final production of co-
emergent bliss and wisdom in enlightenment. Wherever the
Master finds his consorts, his great bliss awakens the
Dakini's natural insight. Saraha, after a long tenure at
Nalanda University, took an arrow-smith's daughter (a
Dakini) as his consort, and said: *Only now am I a truly pure
Bhikshu.*

Drukpa Kunley's life shows us a liberated mind that is
free from the preconceptions, preferences, bias, and mental
activity that bind us in tension and fear, and shows us a way
of life that frees us from emotional attachments and family
ties. He gives us a vision of mad indiscipline and free
wandering, and having accomplished the goal of his
Dharma in one lifetime, he demonstrates a deceptively
simple example and inspiration. His behaviour shows us the

result of the practice of Milarepa's precept: *Concerning the way to pursue your inner search, reject all that increases mind-poisons and clinging to self even though it appears good; and, on the contrary, practice all that counteracts the five mind-poisons, and helps other beings, even though it appears to be bad:* this is essentially in accord with the *Dharma*.

Drukpa Kunley is not only revered by all the Tibetan people. He is so beloved by the Bhutanese that they often like to think that his title refers to a Bhutanese origin rather than the *Drukpa Kahgyu* School. His style, his humour, his earthiness, his compassion, his manner of relating to people, won him a place in the hearts of all the Himalayan peoples – the Sikkimese, the Assamese, the Ladakhis, the Nepalis, the Kunnupas, and the Lahaulis. He may not have been the greatest of scholars or metaphysicians, although he left some beautiful literature behind him, but he is the saint closest to the hearts of the common people, the Buddha to whom they feel most akin. For the common people it was Drukpa Kunley who brought fire down from heaven, and who touched them closest to the bone.

I pray that by spreading this fully enlightened laughter-master's life-story to the ends of the earth, the myriads of beings of the present and the future may draw inspiration from his accomplishments in the *Buddha-Dharma*, so that the dark age may turn into the citadel of Buddhahood.

DUGU CHOEGYAL GYAMTSO
(TULKU)
Full moon of the 2nd month
of the earth sheep year

Translator's Introduction

This sublime and ribald biography of Drukpa Kunley, Tibet's most popular saint, is in the form of an anthology of anecdotes and songs culled from both literary and oral, Tibetan and Bhutanese, sources. It is the work of a contemporary Bhutanese monk and scholar fulfilling the current need of Himalayan Buddhists for a new presentation of Drukpa Kunley's crazy-wisdom. This need arises at a time of rapid change when traditional forms are suspect – much as they were in François Rabelais's France. It appeared to us that the unique ingredients of this hagiography, a positive attitude to sex, an antipathy to organized religion and priestcraft, and the anarchic life-style of an itinerant mystic, would provide an ideal vehicle to carry the Tibetan Buddhist Tradition to those who would never read a formal exposition of the doctrine. In the belief that the significance of *Tantra* has important implications outside the formal system of its practice, and wishing to inform and entertain those already committed to the Tradition, we have taken this opportunity to make a 'secret' biography available to western readers. Hitherto, the reformist oriented holders of the Tantric Lineages have observed the strictures adjuring secrecy of Tantric literature; the unreformed schools have always had a more liberal attitude. Although we expect an adverse reaction from Buddhist schools adhering closely to the Buddha Sakyamuni's teaching in the 'First Turning of the Wheel', we hope that the interest in the *Tantras* this translation excites, the misconceptions that it removes, and the insight and inspiration that it infuses, will vindicate us.

Rabelais' anti-clerical and ribald masterpieces reflected a

new feeling of dissatisfaction with a decadent tradition. Drukpa Kunley's attacks upon monasticism and organized religion are consistent with the spirit of India's perennial *Siddha* tradition. This tradition produced the mystic poet Saraha (Drukpa Kunley was a reincarnation of Saraha) who sang his apocalyptic songs denigrating pious show, academic scholasticism, empty ritual, and self-righteous morality. To this list Drukpa Kunley added profane and feckless monastic sexuality, abuse of authority by privileged hierarchs, exploitation of the ignorant and superstitious, pre-occupation with peripheral religious concerns, wealth, and fame, and many other forms of 'spiritual materialism'. The aim of both Saraha and Drukpa Kunley was to free the human spirit's divinity from slavery to religious institutions, and moral and ritual conventions, that had originally been designed to support spiritual endeavour (see page 109). Both these *Yogins*, as exemplars of the uncompromising, ascetic path, believed that total renunciation and detachment, including detachment from religion and its institutions, were necessary conditions for perfect happiness. In Tibet, the Red-Hat struggle against the centralized, hierarchical theocracy of Lhasa, which began in the 17th century, can be viewed as a conflict between entropic establishmentarian forces and the individual seeking to work out his own salvation. This freedom is the cherished ethos of the Tantric Tradition in general, and the Bhutanese Tradition in particular, which Drukpa Kunley did so much to foster; it is anarchic like the Christianity of the Desert Fathers and the Islam of the Sufis. However, Drukpa Kunley's attacks on the establishment are never vicious. He himself was a product of monastic training (though he grew out of the spiritual nursery at an early age), and he must have realized that the monastery provided a unique haven for those with inferior capabilities and those with different propensities in need of a social environment for their spiritual evolution.

To emphasize the nature of the positive aspect of Drukpa Kunley's mystic path, the Path of *Tantra,* we considered *The Craft of Desire* as a possible alternative title to this translation. Emotion, particularly desire, is not to be suppressed, it is to be purified. And then free of selfish motivation, in fulfilment of the SAMAYA (the pledge to sustain ultimate awareness), it is to be used to bring dis-illusionment, awareness, and delight, to all beings. The stories of Drukpa Kunley's philandering should be read with this in mind, and it will become evident why the craft with which he expressed his desire is irreproachable. To impute prurient motivation to the Adept is to totally misconstrue the dynamic of his existence, and a prurient delight or disgust on the reader's part will indicate a failure to understand one of life's great mysteries and an essential message of the *Tantras*: the blissful nature of all phenomena is realized in the union of duality (subject/object, consciousness/sensory stimuli, male/female). Whether his consort is a human being or a sensory field, the Adept participates in a consummate union of skilful means (male) and awareness (female), compassionate skilful means awakening the awareness potential of the 'Empty' female counterpart. In this union, the Tantric Mysteries, symbolized in *mandalas* of gods and goddesses, are revealed. His sexual activity is only a part of his craft of releasing people from ignorance – the universal psychosis that occludes the Buddha-nature inherent in us all – and eradicating the fixed notions of who we are and what we should and should not do. The genius of his therapeutic craft lies in spontaneous speech and action that awakens awareness of an authentic existential reality. Outrage and laughter are the skilful means he employs to shock people out of their lethargic acceptance of the neurotic *status quo* of their minds, and out of their attachment to conventional forms. All Drukpa Kunley's relationships are determined by the craft of his desire to attain his own and others' simultaneous and continuous enlightenment.

Drukpa Kunley attained Buddhahood as a result of the arduous, highly disciplined training in listening, pondering, and meditating, which he received in the austere environment of the Tibetan monastic academy, following the instructions and precepts, and receiving the authentic inner initiations and empowerments of the Lamas of his school. The Red-Hat, *Drukpa Kahgyu* School (one of the four major *Kahgyu* Schools and intimately related to the *Nyingmapa*) had been established at Ralung in southern Tibet by his ancestor, Palden Drukpa Rimpoche, an initiate of the lineage established by Tilopa, Naropa, Marpa, and Milarepa (see Appendix 2, page 190). But once he had attained his goal, at an exceptionally young age, he transcended the boundaries between the different schools; he became the universal mystic. The monasteries of Drepung, Galden and Tsurphu, which he ridiculed, all recall his visits with great affection. Jealousy of one's chosen method of spiritual evolution functions, initially, like a tin pipe placed over a seedling to protect it from the ravages of sheep or rabbits, but, finally, it becomes necessary for the neophyte to stand alone, free of all social supports and psychic crutches, as the *Guru* demonstrates. This glorious isolation, in the world but not of it, is one definition of the indefinable Great Perfection (*Dzokchen*) and the Magnificent Stance (*Mahamudra, Chakchen*), which outside the schoolroom are synonyms for Drukpa Kunley's spiritual attainment (see pages 113-14).

Drukpa Kunley has become more than an historical figure. In Bhutan he is a culture hero around whom a web of stories and legends, facts and fictions, have been spun. Tibetan beer-house raconteurs use his name interchangeably with the less than holy Agu Tomba, the lewd secular character who recurs in Tibetan folklore to instruct in popular wisdom. But in the abundance of authentic tales told of him, he is the archetypal divine madman, whose personality is formed by the imperatives of the mythic hero of this mode of spiritual being. These imperatives are found embedded in the legends of the Eighty Four Indian *Mahasiddhas*, in the stories of the plethora of divine crazies who appeared during the flowering of the Tibetan Tradition (fourteenth to sixteenth centuries), and even today in Indian villagers' highest expectations of their *Pagala Babas* (mad saints). Care-free renunciation, an excess of compassion, total lack of inhibition, skilful use of shock-therapy, tears and laughter, are the specific characteristics of the divine madman. An itinerant mode of life, practised by a vast variety of people, is socially acceptable throughout the East. If insanity is defined as deviation from a psychological norm, the divine madman is truly crazy; but if a spiritual ideal is used as a yardstick, undoubtedly, it is the vast majority of us who are insane.

A word should be said here on behalf of the Tibetan people. Please do not delude yourselves that they are a bawdy bunch. Although they have few neurotic obsessions regarding sex, they have a strong sense of shame. Tibetan women will blush at the mention of sex and look askance at the 'liberated' western girl. Likewise, monks are inordinately embarrassed by even the milder of Drukpa Kunley's jokes. Even laymen, enjoying his humour hugely, have an acute sense of the time and place. So although, initially, western readers may be shocked to find sex and scripture confounded, Tibetans are probably more sensitive to the therapeutic effect of the stories.

In the second half of this book, Drukpa Kunley is seen in Bhutan preoccupied with a peculiar activity that needs some explanation. In the sixteenth century, the people of Bhutan still lived under the spell of animist superstition, and it was Drukpa Kunley's duty and pleasure to enslave or destroy the 'demons' which cowed the populace. The different species of demons can best be explained as configurations of various natural, elemental forces affecting the minds of human beings, and inseparable from the fear and instinctual responses that they incite. The seat of these forces may be inside the body or without. For example, the demon of a mountain pass can be a conformation of the latent powers of the phenomena of cold, snow, wind, and high altitude, given projected form and character by the common experience and imagination of many fearful, exhausted, and triumphant men crossing the pass. Whether this demon becomes substantialized as a discrete but subtle entity by generations of worshippers is disputable, but certainly it affects them as if it did possess an independent existence. A further example: a serpent-demon can be the latent power of disease or disaster, inherent as a virus or a potentially dangerous ecological imbalence or instability in the elements of earth or water, confounded with the fear and respect, say, that cholera and earthquakes produce. There are many disparate forms of serpent demons, and every demon will be endowed with the peculiar characteristics of its location and the various projections formed by diverse human responses to it. The internal demons that bothered Sakyamuni as he sat under the *Bodhi* Tree are 'simple' demons: the demon 'fear of death', for instance, can be located in states of enervation and depression, and recognized in both thought and emotion as well as in habitual reaction patterns. The shaman, possessed by a demon, is invested with black magical powers. Drukpa Kunley demonstrated not merely how to destroy demons, but how to transform them into guardians and protectors of the Buddhas' Truth. The agent of transformation that effects this miracle is the immutable strength and consistency of the ultimate, transcending awareness of the mind, symbolized herein by Drukpa Kunley's stick with a penis head, or by his own penis (*Vajra, Dorje*), referred to as 'The Flaming Thunderbolt of Wisdom'. The demon takes refuge in Buddha immediately the *Dorje* reveals its Empty nature, and, thereafter, so long as the Master occasionally reminds the demon of his continuous intuitive awareness of demonic apparitions' essential Emptiness, it is tied to his will. What originally were hostile elemental forces, and atavistic fears, are now ferocious masks to frighten interlopers intruding upon the sanctuary of truth, and potent energies capable of performing mundane tasks for the Adept – friendly helpers on the path.

Our hero's full personal name is Kunga Legpa'i Zangpo, which is contracted to Kunga Legpa, or simply Kunleg (Kunley). His title '*Drukpa*' indicates that he belongs to the *Drukpa Kahgyu* School, and that he is associated with Bhutan. 'Master of Truth' (*Chos-rje*) indicates his mastery of the *Dharma*, the Buddhas' Law and its practice. 'Lord of Beings' ('*Gro-ba'i mgon-po*) is an epithet of the Bodhisattva of Compassion as the liberator of gods, men, titans, beasts, hungry ghosts, and fiends. Since he is a Buddha, and Guru Preceptor, to numerous of his contemporaries, and to his disciples of succeeding generations, he is called 'Lama'. The title '*Naljorpa*' (*Yogin* in Sanskrit, *Yogi* in the vernacular) identifies him as an itinerant renunciate and Adept proficient in meditation and magical manipulation; literally,

Naljorpa (rnal-'byor-pa) means 'he who is tied to serenity', 'he who adheres to an authentic personal reality', or 'he who is an embodiment of the union of male and female principles'. 'Adept' is a rendering of *Druptop (siddha)*, one who has gained both relative magical powers and realization of reality's ultimate nature. The last of Drukpa Kunley's epithets, *Jadral (bya-bral)*, which I have rather flippantly translated as 'Duty-Free', means that he abides in the free-space of *Mahamudra*, wherein action is called Non-Action: his motion is in such harmony with the universe that it requires no effort or striving; spontaneous and uninhibited, it transcends our concepts of work or activity. Three other titles, often misunderstood, deserve definition. 'Precious One' (*Rimpoche*) is the form that devotees use to address their Lama, and serfs used to address their ecclesiastical overlords. '*Tulku*' (Incarnation) has a profound metaphysical reality – it indicates the transforming emanation of the Buddha-Essence – and in a political context it denominates the titular head of a monastery. '*Gomchen*', for which I have been unable to find a pithy equivalent, is the name given to an ascetic meditator who spends his life, or the major part of it, in a cave or hut, often sealed, in the jungle or a Himalayan fastness.

The Tibetan text ('*Gro-ba'i mgon-po chos-rje kun-dga' legs-pa'i rnam-thar rgya-mtsho'i snying-po mthong-ba don-ldan*) was compiled in 1966 by one of Bhutan's most learned authorities on Drukpa Kunley, Geshey Chaphu (*dGe-shes Brag-phug dge-'dun rin-chen*). He wrote it at Kunga Choling, a lovely hermitage below Sangchen Chokhor in the Paro Valley in Bhutan. In accordance with traditional Tibetan practice, his first draft was circulated amongst his scholarly colleagues, notably the Lopons Nado, Pema, and Kunley, for them to edit. Thus, we may be reasonably certain of the authenticity of the stories, and that they did indeed originate in the sixteenth century. Lopon Nado was responsible for the revised printed edition published in Kalimpong (West Bengal) that we, the translators, have utilized. The Kalimpong edition has proved very popular among Tibetan-speaking people.

About the translation: our overriding aim has been to

reflect the tenor of the *Naljorpa*'s life in an idiom equivalent to that of the original text. Thus, far from attempting a literal translation, in order to elucidate obscurities in both primary meaning and connotation, and to achieve cogent English prose, inevitable omission and interpretative amplification have been made. Apart from passages and songs explicitly treating Tantric teaching, and requiring scrupulous care and attention, the translation has been made in the light of the interpretation of an educated layman. Sonam Paljor's help was indispensable, particularly in dealing with the idiom in which the text abounds. Other points to note: repeated vulgarisms have been translated euphemistically; words such as 'Emptiness' (*Sunyata*) and 'Empty' (*Sunya*) that lack the richness of the original term have been given a distinguishing capital letter; proper names have been put into approximate phonetics and translated only when meaning is added; and Bhutanese place names have been given their modern form, and an indication of their location has been added in brackets where necessary. We apologize to the spirit of Drukpa Kunley for any lapse in translation of his inimitable puns, nuance, and humour, and any failing to convey the multi-levelled meaning of his *Dharma*.

I am very grateful for Geshey Chaphu's permission to translate this work; to Drukpa Tuktse Rimpoche (the tutor to the Drukchen who is the supreme Lama of the *Drukpa Kahgyu* School) for his blessing upon the work and his encouragement of it, at Hemis, Ladakh; to Choegyal Rimpoche of Tashi Jong, Kangra Valley, who as a lineal descendant of Drukpa Kunley has written the foreword and given me invaluable encouragement; to my friend, Sonam Paljor, a layman of Kathmandu, with whom with great pleasure I read the text; and to Hal Kuloy for introducing me to the text and providing the impetus for translation; to Lee Baarslag for her illustrations done in a very short time; and to Lobzang Gyamtso, Choje Rimpoche, Peter Cooper, Linda Wellings, and my wife and all those who made this book possible.

KEITH DOWMAN (KUNZANG TENZIN)
Kathmandu, Nepal

The Divine Madman

Prologue

NAMO GURU BAY!
Drukpa Kunley, the Master of Truth, himself said,
'If you think I have revealed any secrets, I apologize;
If you think this a medley of nonsense, enjoy it!'
Such sentiments, here, I fully endorse.

The Great Master of Yoga, Kunga Legpai Palzangpo, was a reincarnation of the Adepts Saraha and Shavaripa[1] who had lived in India, the Land of the Saints. His essential nature was the all-embracing field of Ultimate Reality. Free of passionate impulses, his virtue fully matured, he was a manifest Buddha, constituting in himself an infinitude of perfected capabilities. Through his pre-eminently skilful dance of life, controlling every situation for the sake of all beings, he demonstrated his knowledge of the identity of Samsara and Nirvana.[2] Without any equivocation he revealed the magical signs of his accomplishment to the public eye; and due to his unfailing intuition of delusory appearances as a lie, he was free of all hypocrisy and deceit. Through spontaneous execution and care-free enjoyment of whatever it befell him to perform, he created immense space and freedom in his mind; and since he had destroyed all partiality in himself and shared his love equally with all beings, he found himself a homeless renunciate. In a casual encounter with him, people would abandon their attachments to the outer show of this world like tattered rags.

On the surface, these stories report the activity of a man of the world, but, ultimately, they reflect an inner life which conforms to the Sutras, Tantras,[3] and the Lama's precepts. This revelation of a white magician's wisdom is like a drop of ambrosia to be received upon the tip of a stalk of the kusha grass of faith, a droplet taken from the ocean of scriptural accounts of the Adept's awakening, capable of setting a seed of liberation in the stream of consciousness merely by reading it. The Master himself abundantly documented his life in his Collected Works, Instructions and miscellaneous writings. This autobiographical material, augmented by faithful patrons' written compositions of the elders' oral tradition, has been edited into a potpourri in eight chapters subtitled, 'Behold Her and Laugh!'

To begin with, to explain the subject matter, if you ask for a taste of these stories regarding incompatibility: water and butter are incompatible, blood and milk do not mix, dust disagrees with the eye, thorns are unwelcome in the sole of the foot, a large penis is uncongenial to a small virgin, and falsehood is inimical to the Holy Scriptures. Likewise, the casual indifference that you show for the earth under your feet is incompatible with the Sacred Teaching – you must read these stories with reverent attention and faith. Further, if you ask for a taste of this biography as regards 'leaking' when you read it: if you read it with shame you will perspire, if you read it with deep faith you will weep; if you read it with languor you will drool at the mouth; if a woman reads it with lust her lotus flower will moisten; and if anyone reads it and distorts it with an opinionated mind, his soul will leak into the lower realms. Accordingly, those individuals who have no reverence for the Path of Tantra by virtue of their ignorance of Tantric strictures and prohibitions, and those who despise discipline, should not read it. If those who do not understand that the original nature of mind is to be perceived in the essence of the Insight/Skilful Means union read it, they will sicken at the unadorned talk of private parts, talk that is inimical to their faith in the Buddhas' Teaching. So it is imperative that you do not sit lackadaisically in attitudes of disrespect, that you do not laugh raucously at dirty jokes, and that you keep your minds awake, refraining from indulging in interpretive fantasies. Listen in relaxation with a clear mind.

1 How Drukpa Kunley became an Ascetic Wanderer and how he delivered the Lady Sumchokma from the Ocean of Suffering

We bow at the feet of Kunga Legpa,
Possessor of the bow and arrow that slays the Ten Enemies,
Master of the hunting dog that kills dualizing tendencies,
And Bearer of the Shield of Loving Kindness, Compassion,
and Patience.

The Naljorpa,[4] Drukpa Kunley, came from an extremely exalted family and spiritual lineage. In latter day Buddhist India, there were many great Adepts, foremost of whom was Narotapa.[5] Narotapa decided to gain rebirth in the Land of the Snows to spread the teaching that gives meaning and purpose to people's lives. In that land of the Bodhisattva Lotus-in-Hand,[6] near Yagyal in the east of the province of Tsang, over the pass of the Mountain-Demon Complete Contentment, in a place called Nyangto Saral, there was a large nomad encampment. In that camp lived a man named Zurpo Tsape of the family of Gya[7] with his wife, Maza Darkyi. Narotapa entered the womb of Maza Darkyi, and was born the youngest of her seven sons, all of whom were destined to become the pride of the land. This particularly blessed youngest son was to be called the Peerless, the Sun of the Land of Snows, Master of Truth, Lord of Beings, Palden Drukpa Rimpoche.[8]

Palden Drukpa Rimpoche was born in the year of the female-iron-snake in the third cycle (1161 AD), the year of the Royal Bull.[9] His elder brother, the Son of Lhabum, begat the Preceptor Bontak, who begat Dorje Lingpa Senge Sherab, and the Exalted Layman, Senge Rinchen. Senge Rinchen begat the Great Thirteenth of the lineage, Senge Gyalpo, who begat Jamyang Kunga Senge, who begat the

Master of Truth, Sherab Senge, and an emanation of the
Bodhisattva of Intelligence, Yeshe Rinchen. Yeshe Rinchen
begat an emanation of the Lord of the Mysteries, Namkha
Palzang, an emanation of the Bodhisattva of Compassion,
Sherab Zangpo, and the Attendant, Dorje Gyalpo. Dorje
Gyalpo begat the Official, Rinchen Zangpo. This Rinchen
Zangpo, descended from such an august line, was the
husband of Gonmokyi, who gave birth to the Master of
Truth, Kunga Legpai Zangpo,[10] in the year of the wood-pig
in the eighth cycle (1455 AD).

The Master of Truth, Kunga Legpa was extremely pre-
cocious. With full memory of his previous life, he imitated
Naljorpas in meditation, he practised breathing exercises,
and yoga was his full preoccupation. These signs produced
great faith in his family and devotees. By his third year, he
could read with ease. When he was older, his father was
assassinated in a family feud, and disillusioned with the
world, he decided to enter upon the religious life. Leaving
his home, patrimony, family, and friends, as though they
were so much dust under his feet, he took the precepts of
layman and novice from Lama Nenying Choje. Later, he
received ordination as a monk from Jekhyen Rabpa of
Zhalu. The monk Sonam Chokpa taught him the Esoteric
Tantras of the Secret Mantra Tradition, while at the Lotus
Feet of Gyalwong Je, he learnt the complete doctrine of the
Drukpa Tradition, concentrating upon the Three Secret
Teachings[11] of Palden Drukpa Rimpoche, the founder of his
spiritual lineage. At the Lotus Feet of the Sage Lhatsun
Chempo and others who combined meditative realization
with dialectic skill he heard and assimilated the teaching of
the entire Doctrine, and attained realization of the inner
meaning of the Four Initiations and Empowerments.[12] He
went on to absorb the secret treasury of initiation, precept,
and advice of many other Lamas.

Through a synthesis of the meaning of all the oral instruction he had received, he discovered the key to all realization:
BE AWARE! GUARD THE MIND! Upon this understanding,
he offered his robes to the image of Buddha, and as a
mendicant wandering wherever he would, he abandoned
systematic yoga and meditation. He summarized his under-

standing in these verses:

> 'Failing to catch the spirit of the Buddhas,
> What use is it to follow the letter of the Law?
> Without an apprenticeship to a competent Master,
> What use is great talent and intelligence?
> Unable to love all beings as your sons,
> What use is solemn prayer and ritual?
> Ignorant of the sole point of the Three Vows,[13]
> What is gained by breaking each in turn?
> Failing to realize that Buddha is within,
> What reality can be found outside?
> Incapable of a natural stream of meditation,
> What can be gained by violating thought?
> Unable to regulate life according to the seasons and the
> time of the day,
> Who are you but a muddled, indiscrimate fool?
> If an enlightened perspective is not intuitively grasped,
> What can be gained by a systematic search?
> Living on borrowed time and energy, wasting your life,
> Who will repay your debts in the future?
> Wearing coarse and scanty clothing in great discomfort,
> What can the ascetic gain by suffering the cold hells in this life?
> The aspirant striving without specific instruction,
> Like an ant climbing a sand hill, accomplishes nothing.
> Gathering instruction, but ignoring meditation on the nature
> of mind,
> Is like starving oneself when the larder is full.
> The sage who refuses to teach or write,
> Is as useless as the jewel in the King Snake's head.
> The fool who knows nothing but prattles constantly,
> Merely proclaims his ignorance to all.
> Understanding the essence of the Teaching,[14] practise it!'

By the age of twenty-five, Kunga Legpa had gained mastery of both mundane and spiritual arts. He was accomplished in the arts of prescience, shape-shifting, and magical display. Returning home to visit his mother in Ralung,[15] she failed to recognize his achievement and judged him merely by his outward behaviour.

'You must decide exactly who you are,' she complained. 'If you decide to devote yourself to the religious life, you must work constantly for the good of others. If you are going to be a lay householder, you should take a wife who can help your old mother in the house.'

Now the Naljorpa was instinctively guided at all times by his vow to dedicate his sight, his ears, his mind, and his sensibility, to others on the path, and knowing that the time was ripe to demonstrate his crazy yet compassionate wisdom, he replied immediately, 'If you want a daughter-in-law, I'll go and find one.'

He went straight to the market place, where he found a hundred-year-old hag with white hair and blue eyes, who was bent at the waist and had not so much as a single tooth in her head. 'Old lady,' he said, 'today you must be my bride. Come with me!'

The old woman was unable to rise, but Kunley put her on his back, and carried her home to his mother.

'O Ama! Ama!' he called to her. 'You wanted me to take a wife, so I've just brought one home.'

'If that's the best that you can do, forget it,' moaned his mother. 'Take her back where she came from or you'll find yourself looking after her. I could do her work better than she.'

'All right,' said Kunley with studied resignation. 'If you can do her work for her, I'll take her back.' And he returned her to the market place.

Nearby lived the exalted abbot Ngawong Chogyal,[16] an incarnation of the Bodhisattva of Compassion[17] as a chaste and holy man who sincerely practised the Creative and Fulfilment Stages[18] of meditation. During a break in his devotions he thought to himself, 'The house belonging to Kunga Legpa and his mother needs some improvement. Every lay devotee should have a shrine room, and while we're about it we could add a latrine. Now where should we build the latrine? The east side of the house is definitely unappealing. The south side seems rather unsuitable. The west is saline, and the north is infested with angry spirits. . . .'

As Ngawong Chogyal was deliberating uncertainly in this manner, Kunley returned from the market place. His mother greeted him with this admonition, 'A good son should be like Ngawong Chogyal. See how he serves the monks, returns the kindness of his parents, works for the welfare of all beings, and keeps himself spiritually pure. He's a true servant of the people!'

'And yet your Ngawong Chogyal can't even decide where to build a latrine!' laughed the Lama.

That night Kunley went to his mother's bed carrying his blanket.

'What do you want?' asked his mother.

'This morning you said you'd perform a wife's duties, didn't you?' he replied.

'You shameless creature!' responded his mother. 'I said I'd do her housework. Now don't be so stupid. Go back to your own bed.'

'You should have said what you meant this morning,' the Lama told her, lying down. 'It's too late now. We are going to sleep together.'

'Shut up and go away, you miserable man!' she swore at him.

'My knee has gone bad and I can't get up. You'd better resign yourself to it,' he persisted.

'Even if you've no shame,' she said, 'what will other people think? Just imagine the gossip!'

'If you're afraid of gossip, we can keep it a secret,' he promised.

Finally, unable to find words to rebuff him, she said, 'You don't have to listen to me, just don't tell anyone else. Anyhow, there's a proverb that goes, "To sell your body, you don't need a pimp; to hang a painted scroll you don't need a nail; and to wither your virtue, you don't need a mat in the sun." So do it if you're going to!'

Her words fell into his ears like water into boiling ghee, and he sprang up and left her alone.

Early next morning he went down to the market place and shouted aloud, 'Hey listen, you people! If you persist, you can seduce even your own mother!' When the whole crowd was aghast, he left. But by exposing the hidden foibles of his mother, her faults were eradicated, her sins expiated, and her troubles and afflictions removed. She went on to live to the ripe old age of one hundred and thirty years.

Soon after this incident, he told his mother that he was going to Lhasa, and that in the future he would live the life of a Naljorpa.

Then the Master of Truth, Lord of Beings, Kunga Legpa, wandered to Lhasa as an itinerant Naljorpa. The market place of the capital was as crowded as the night sky is with stars. He found there Indians, Chinese, Newars, Ladakhis, and Tibetans from the Northern Highlands, together with people from Kham, Mongolia, Central Tibet, Tsang, Dakpo, Kongpo, the cis-Himalayas and representatives of every valley in the country. Nomads, farmers, Lamas, officers, monks, nuns, Naljorpas, devotees, traders, and pilgrims were all gathered together in the Holy City.

'Listen to me, all you people!' shouted the Lama. 'I am Drukpa Kunley of Ralung, and I have come here today, without prejudice, to help you all. Where can I find the best chung[19] and the most beautiful women? Tell me!'

The crowd was startled, and muttered to one another, 'This madman says he's come here for the sake of all beings and then asks where he can find alcohol and women! What kind of piety is that? He should be asking who is the greatest Lama, which is the most desirable monastery, and where is religion flourishing most strongly. But he has no such questions. Most likely he's the type of religious freak who binds girls to the Wheel of Truth rather than demons!'

There was a man in the crowd with a white skin, a sooty face, a head like a blacksmith's hammer, staring bulging eyes, lips like a sheep's intestines, a forehead like an up-turned begging bowl, and a neck as thin as a horse's tail with a vast goitre growing out of it. He shouted back at the Lama, 'You may try to tell us you're a man, you idiot, but you surely have no home; you may tell us you're a bird, but you have no perch; you may call yourself a deer, but you have no forest; you may call yourself a beast, but you have no lair; you may call yourself a devotee, but you have no sect; you may call yourself a monk, but you have no monastery; you may call yourself a Lama, but you have no throne. You troublesome, presumptuous beggar! In the day time you pick nits, and in the night time you get drunk and

steal other men's wives to play with. You are no holy man.
If you were, you would have a spiritual lineage. Tell us your
spiritual lineage!'

'Oh you mad dog! Sit down and keep quiet!' Kunley
shouted in reply. 'You want to know my origin and birth?
You want to know my spiritual lineage? Listen then, and I
will tell you.'[20]

> 'This vagrant's lineage is highly exalted,
> It descends from the Vajra Bearer!
> This vagrant's Lama is truly exalted,
> His name is Lama Palden Drukpa!
> This vagrant's Deity is truly exalted,
> His name is Supreme Delight!
> This vagrant's Dakini is truly exalted,
> Her name is Diamond Sow-Face!
> This vagrant's Protector is truly exalted,
> His name is the Great Four-Armed Black One!'

When he had finished this verse his accuser was silent and
slunk away. Then an ancient man from Lhasa arose from
the crowd and prostrated to the Lama before singing this
song:

> 'Glorious Drukpa Kunley!
> I live in the City of Lhasa
> And Lhasa is famed for its beautiful women.
> It's impossible to name them all
> But here are the names of the best of them:
> Palzang Buti, Wongchuk Tsewong Zangpo,
> Kalzang Pemo, Smiling Sangyay Gyalmo,
> Sonam Dronma, Dancing Chokyi Wongmo,
> And the Lamp of Lhasa Don Akyi.
> Such are their names and there's countless others.
> And you'll find good chung in Lhasa.
> Is this to your liking, Naljorpa?'

Kunley replied, 'It seems that Lhasa is full of beautiful
women and good chung. I'll enjoy your town sometime!'

Then an old man from Sakya stood up and sang this song:

> 'Glorious Kunga Legpa!
> I am from the Land of Sakya
> Where the beauty of the women is legendary.
> It's impossible to name them all

But here are the names of our finest:
Asal Pemo, the maiden Gakyi,
Bumo Andruk, Lhacho Wongmo,
Asa Tsering Drolma
Dekyi Saldon, and Dasal Yangkyi.
Such are their names and there's many more besides.
And we have excellent chung in Sakya.
Does this appeal to you Naljorpa?'

'Yah! Yah!' said the Lama. 'I'll go to Sakya some day.'
Then an old man, this time from Ladakh, stood up and
said his piece:

'Glorious Kunga Legpa!
I come from the Land of Ladakh
Where beautiful women are honoured.
If you ask me their names, I'll mention
Tsewong Lhadron, the maiden Chokyi,
The Highland Girl Atsong Bumo.
Lhachik Buti, Ama Akyi,
Karma Dechen Pemo, and Sonam Gyalmo –
Such are the names to remember.
We also have fine chung in Ladakh.
Will you come there to taste it Naljorpa?'

'Yah! Yah!' said the Naljorpa. 'I'll come to Ladakh some
day!'
Next, an old woman from Bhutan arose and said, 'You
Tibetans talk too much! The Naljorpa's name is Drukpa[21]
Kunley not Tibetan Kunley!' And she sang this song:

'Glorious Drukpa Kunley!
I am from the Land of Bhutan
Which is full of sought-after beauties.
I cannot name all of our women
But here are some to remember:
Gokyi Palmo is the Dakini of Woche,
The Lady Adzom is the Dakini of Gomyul Sar Stupa,
Namkha Dronma of Pachang is the Dakini of Zhung Valley,
Palzang Buti is the Dakini of the Zhung Highlands,
Chodzom is the Dakini of Barpaisa in Wongyul,
Samten Tsemo, Lama Nyida Drakpa's daughter, is the
    Dakini of Paro,
Mistress Gyaldzom is the Dakini of Shar Khyungtsei
    Chanden. . . .

There are some names and there are countless others besides.
And we too have excellent chung.
Does Bhutan appeal to you, Naljorpa?'

'Yah! Yah!' said the Yogin. 'One day I'll visit Bhutan and drink your chung and enjoy your women!'

Finally, an old woman from Kongpo had her say:

'O glorious Kunga Legpa!
I am from the Land of Kongpo
And these are the names of our belles:
Lhacho Pemo, the maiden Palzang,
Rinchen Gyalmo, Tsewong Gyalmo,
Tenzin Zangmo, Tseten Lhamo,
And Virgin Sumchok.
These are some of their names
        And there are numerous others besides. . . .
And we, also, have first class chung.
Won't you visit Kongpo, Naljorpa?'

'Yah! Yah!' said the Naljorpa. 'It seems that even in Kongpo there are many beautiful women. But it's not sufficient merely to know of their existence, one must see and experience them oneself. In particular, the girl called Sumchok interests me. How old is she?'

'She's fifteen,' replied the Kongpo woman.

'Then I must go there quickly before it's too late', said the Lama. 'Stay well all of you! I must go and find Sumchok!'

As the Lama was leaving Nyerong behind him on his way to Kongpo (a province south-east of Lhasa), he encountered five girls on the road.

'Where are you from and where are you going?' they asked him.

'I come from behind me and I'm going on ahead', he smiled.

'Please answer our questions', begged the girls. 'Why are you travelling?'

'I am looking for a fifteen year old girl', the Lama told them. 'She has a fair complexion and soft, silky, warm flesh, a tight, foxy and comfortable pussy, and a round smiling face; she is beautiful to behold, sweet to smell, and she has a sharp intuition. In fact she has all the signs of a Dakini.'[22]

'Are we not Dakinis?' asked the girls.

'I doubt it,' replied the Lama. 'You don't appear to be. But there are many types of Dakini.'

'What are they?' they wanted to know.

'The Wisdom Dakini, the Diamond Dakini, the Jewel Dakini, the Lotus Dakini, the Action Dakini, the Buddha Dakini, the Flesh-Eating Dakini, the Worldly Dakini, the Ashen Dakini, and many others.'

'How can one recognize them?' they asked.

'The Wisdom Dakini is fair, flushed and radiant,' the Lama told them. 'She has five white moles across her hair line, and she is compassionate, pure, virtuous and devout. Also, her body is shapely. Coupling with her brings happiness in this life, and prevents any fall into hell in the next. The Buddha Dakini has a bluish complexion and a radiant smile. She has little lust, is long-lived, and bears many sons. Coupling with her bestows longevity and a rebirth in the Orgyen Paradise.[23] The Diamond Dakini is fair with a well-filled supple body. She has long eyebrows, a sweet voice, and enjoys singing and dancing. Coupling with her brings success in this life and rebirth as a god. The Jewel Dakini has a pretty white face with a pleasant yellow tinge to it. Her body is slender, and she is tall. Her hair is white, and she has little vanity and a very slender waist line. Coupling with her gives one wealth in this life, and shuts the gates of hell. The Lotus Dakini has a bright pink skin, an oily complexion, a short body and limbs, and wide hips. She is lustful and garrulous. Coupling with her generates many sons, while gods, demons and men are controlled, and the gates to the lower realms are closed. The Action Dakini has a radiant blue skin with a brownish hue, and a broad forehead. She is rather sadistic. Coupling with her is a defence against enemies, and closes the gates to the lower realms. The Worldly Dakini has a white, smiling, and radiant face, and she is respectful to her parents and friends. She is trustworthy and a generous spender. Coupling with her assures one of the continuance of the family line, generates food and wealth, and assures one of rebirth as a human being. The Flesh-Eating Dakini has a dark and ashen complexion, a wide mouth with protruding fangs, a trace of a third eye upon her forehead, long claw-like finger nails, and a black heart in her vagina. She delights in eating meat, and she devours the children that she bears. Also, she is an insomniac. Coupling with her induces a short life, much disease, little enjoyment of wealth in this life, and rebirth in the deepest hell. The Ashen Dakini has yellow flesh which has an ashen complexion and a spongy texture. She eats ashes from the grate. Coupling with her causes much suffering and enervation, and rebirth as a hungry ghost.'

'What kind of Dakinis are we?' asked the girls eagerly.

'You are a rather different kind,' replied the Lama.

'What type?' they insisted.

'You are greedy but poor, and sexually frustrated but friendless. Even if you do find some idiot to couple with you, no one will gain anything from it.'

The girls were deeply offended by the Lama's words, and went on their way sulking.

Henceforth, the Lama carried a bow and arrow – representing Penetrating Insight and Skilful Means[24] – to slay the Ten Enemies of the Ten Directions;[25] and he led a hunting dog to hunt and kill the habit of dualistic thinking. His long hair was gathered behind his head and tied there; while from his ears hung large round rings. He covered his torso with a vest and the lower part of his body with a cotton skirt.

When he arrived in Kongpo, the Land of Ravines, the Lama sat down in front of the Chieftain Ox-Head's castle and leaned against a prayer-flag pole. Having assured himself that no one else was in the vicinity, he sang this song to awaken Sumchok (Three Jewels):

'In this happy land of U, paradise of prosperity and plenty,
Immured within this mean fortress-prison of Samsara,[26]
Sumchok! charming virgin nymph,
Stop a moment and listen to me –
A Naljorpa who aimlessly wanders abroad
Sings verses with hidden meanings to you.

'Way up in the vast vault of the young night sky
The strong light of the white full moon
Extinguishes creatures' darkness.
But surely the Dragon Planet is jealous.
Say he is free from envy and jealousy
And let me remove the gloom of the Four Continents.

'In the garden of heavenly delight, thick with blooms
   of various hues,
The flower that radiates bright scarlet light
Harbours the honey sucked by the bee.
But surely Drought and Hail are jealous.
Say they are free from envy and jealousy
And let me make an offering to the Three Jewels.

'Here, paramount in Kongpo, in the centre of U,
Sumchok, child of Kongpo, born of Emptiness,
If our bodies were to join in love
Surely Ox-Head would be jealous.
Say he is free from envy and jealousy
And let Sumchok awake a little and grow into Buddhahood.'

Sumchok was serving tea to the Chieftain when she heard
the Lama's song quite clearly. Arising, she looked from a
window, and as if in a vision, the beggar leaning against the
flag pole appeared as the rising fifteen day old moon.
Immediately she saw him her heart filled with devotion.
Although she had never seen him before, since she had
heard the name of Drukpa Kunley and heard stories of his
signs of accomplishment and great skill in magical transformation, she recognized him. And she sang this song back
to him:

'Beggar, sitting in the wide green mountain meadow,
Full moon beggar, listen to me!
Your ashen body hides a Buddha's heart
And your naked body radiates glorious effulgence;
A small shield of patience is slung on your back
And you carry bow and arrow as Insight and Means;
You lead a dog to hunt confusing emotion
And you control the Three Realms[27] with your ascetic yoga.
You are either a shape-shifting demon
Or an Adept with miraculous powers –
You seem too good to be true!

'A moon-faced beggar leaning against the prayer-flag pole. . . .'

'But if your currency is valid,
Look at this poor piece of iron on the blacksmith's anvil,
Hammered by the smith at whim,
Caught by pincers, unable to escape.
If you are truly a skilled blacksmith's son,
Do not leave me on this anvil forever,
But fashion me into a lock of the Jowo Temple;[28]
The karma of iron exhausted
Let me gain Buddhahood.

'Look at this meanest piece of wood, this doorstep,
Trampled upon by dogs and swine,
Held firmly in place by the doorposts.
If you are truly a skilled carpenter's son,
Do not leave me a doorstep forever,
But shape me into a lintel for the Jowo Temple;
The karma of wood exhausted
Let me gain Buddhahood.

'Look at Sumchok, the unhappiest of women!
Ox-Head's blows make my life unbearable,
But attachment to my world constrains me;
If you are truly a Buddha Lama,
Do not leave me in the mire of Samsara,
But take me with you wherever you go
And let Sumchok gain Buddhahood.'

Kunley and Sumchok, singing their songs back and forth
to each other, were overheard by Ox-Head.
'What is that singing I hear?' he called.
Sumchok with a sharp native wit replied immediately,
'My Lord, here's a beggar with a fine voice at the door, and
he's been singing me the news.'
'What news has he been telling you?' she was asked.
'Apparently hunters have killed some animals in the
mountains today,' she replied. 'And probably, if you went
up there yourself, as the meat has not yet been distributed,
you could bring as much as a hundred carcasses back with
you. If you're lucky you will not need to go without meat
with your tsampa.'[29]
This was like refreshing rain in the desert to the ear of the
Chieftain. 'If that is so, prepare provisions for a seven day
journey for myself and thirty servants,' he ordered.

Sumchok obeyed him instantly. After he had departed, the girl invited the Lama into the parlour and began to prepare tea.

'There will be plenty of opportunity to serve me your brand of tea later,' said the Lama. 'Prepare me this special brew which I have carried all the way from the market in Lhasa! It's ready immediately!' And he caught her by the hand, laid her down on the Chieftain's bed, lifted her chuba and gazed upon her nether mandala. Placing his organ against the piled white lotus mandala between the smoother-than-cream white flesh of her thighs, and having seen that their connection was tightly made, he consummated their union. Making love to her, he gave her more pleasure and satisfaction than she had ever experienced.

'O Sumchok! now serve me your tea,' said the Lama when he had done. She brought him tea, the first strainings of chung, together with meat and tsampa, and everything that his heart desired. Finally he got up to leave, 'It is best if you stay here, Sumchok,' he said. 'I must go now.'

Sumchok, with undivided faith, prostrated before him. 'Don't leave this unfortunate girl in this mess. Take me with you,' she begged.

'I have no time to waste with you,' he told her. 'I will remember you and return to you again.' But Sumchok pleaded with him insistently. 'Since you refuse to remain behind, remember this,' he warned her. 'The mind of a Naljorpa is as inconsistent as a madman's babble; it is like rumour of distant events, and like a whore's bum. If I leave you alone, under a tree or beside a rock, will you stay there?'

'I will obey you in all things,' Sumchok promised.

Then the Lama, knowing that it was destined, took her with him. Coming to a cavern that had a black entrance shaped like a recumbent lion high up upon the valley side, he said to her, 'Sumchok, you must stay here for three years.'

'I'm afraid of this place,' she whispered.

'Then stay here for only three months,' he compromised.

'You said that you would take me with you wherever you went,' she whined. But finally, in order to keep her promise of obedience, she agreed to stay for seven days.

'If you're afraid, go into the cavern, and I'll seal up the entrance,' he advised her. So leaving her inside, he built a rock wall across the cave mouth. At his departure Sumchok sang this song:

> 'Listen Drukpa Kunley!
> Fluff blows away on the breeze
> And catches upon the top of a tree;
> Don't blame the pleasant breeze
> When the fluff is so weightless!
> Dead wood swept away upon the stream's swell
> Bobs up and down upon the water;
> Don't blame the river
> When the wood is so buoyant!
> This Sumchok, begotten in Kongpo,
> Grieved at the sight of the cave;
> Don't blame yourself, Drukpa Kunley,
> When my resolution is so weak!'

'I don't want to hear about your moods,' Kunley told her. 'When I have gone, gods and Dakinis will befriend you in the daytime, and butterlamps and incense will calm you at night. Meditate praying to me continuously.' And with this advice, he left her for Samye.

Through a happy combination of the Lama's compassion and her own devotion, Sumchok gained contentment. Absorbed in the sound of the gods and Dakinis by day, and the smell of incense and the light of butterlamps by night, she had no thought of food for the first three days. On the dawning of the fourth day, she gained release from all frustration in a Body of Light, attaining Buddhahood.[30]

2 How Drukpa Kunley visited Samye and Lhasa for the Sake of All Beings

We bow at the feet of Drukpa Kunga Legpa,
Naked and unadorned, free from tainted awareness,
Free from attachment to his mind or his environment,
Through his craziness taming the perverse and faithless,
Guiding them to spiritual freedom through every sensation.

The Master of Truth, Drukpa Kunley, journeyed from Kongpo to Samye.[1] He arrived there at the time of the great religious festival called Dodechopa.[2] Lamas, professors, Naljorpas, spiritual counsellors, monks, and laymen had gathered there from all over the country; the literate people of Tibet had assembled to fulfil their various religious duties. Some made prostration, others circumambulation. Some performed rites of Vow Restoration,[3] Exorcism,[4] or Destruction of Evil Forces.[5]

'Everybody seems to be performing their religious duties,' said Kunley, 'Since I am also an initiate, I should join in.'

'What rite will you perform?' they asked him.

'I don't have the materials necessary to perform a Sacramental Rite of Offering to the Buddhas and Protectors,[6] and I'm too lazy to do prostration or circumambulation, so 'I'll make a spontaneous Vow Restoration.' And he recited this:

'Indivisible Bliss and Emptiness, Ultimate Awareness,
Renews the bond with the Lama and Deity;
The life-breath of the Vow Violators of the Ten Spheres
Renews the commitment of the Protectors and Guardians;[7]
A pure offering of the Three White Things and the Three
    Sweet Things[8]

Renews the commitment of the Guardian Goddesses;
The offering of a little food, incense and chung
Renews the commitment of Daemons and War gods;
Offerings of hundreds and thousands of gifts
Renew the commitment of self-seeking Lamas;
Offerings of small gifts to the monastery
Satisfy the common attendant disciples;
The gift of a flattering smile
Satisfies the minds of faithless monks;
Withholding from the monks offerings for the future dead
Satisfies the minds of the aged and infirm;
Double and triple offerings for Provost and Steward
Satisfy monastic officials;
An unending string of dry words
Satisfies the ambition of scholars;
False meditation in a fool's paradise
Satisfies the minds of uninstructed Gomchens;[9]
Knocking on doors and the barking of dogs
Satisfy foul-mouthed beggars;
The radiant smile of the youthful Gomchen
Satisfies the minds of the nuns;
Generous funeral donations of tea
Satisfy the lazy shaved-heads;
Superficial flattery
Satisfies politicians and superiors;
Unfulfilled promises
Satisfy shameless servants;
Barren fields
Satisfy serfs;
His own talk, though it fall on empty ears,
Satisfies the garrulous head of the family;
The prattle of harmless drunkards
Satisfies spineless young men;
Master and servants' disputed wealth
Satisfies the scheming steward;
Sugar and butter sweets
Satisfy fat mothers;
Saleable, movable household goods
Satisfy drunken fathers;
Wailing and playing in ashes and dung
Satisfy spoilt children;
The undiscriminating bachelor
Satisfies insatiate women;

'He travelled to Lhasa as a Naljorpa. . . .'

Skill in finding excuses for greed
Satisfies fat bellies;
Cold tea and sour chung
Satisfy uninvited, hungry guests;
A fresh breeze blowing from the mountains
Satisfies weaving girls prevented from working;
Uncooked and unsalted radish
Satisfies lazy servants and labourers;
A pot covered with a coat of lacquer
Satisfies potters turning leaking pots;
Snot, phlegm and mucus
Satisfy makers of spitoons.'

The people who heard this were quite astonished. An old man from Kham, full of reverence and devotion, prostrated before him. 'Precious Master of Truth, your words are truly a great blessing! Would you be so kind as to recite a liturgy of Destruction of Evil Forces and Pacification of Obstructing Spirits?' he begged.

The Lama obliged:

'Ho! Perfected Buddha of Every Possibility,
Arisen from the measureless Emptiness of illusion,
Accept an offering of my destiny
And dissolve all mental chatter.
Worldly attachment and ambition
Are the bane of every Lama –
Destroy it by meditating upon the purity of all phenomena.
Disciples who keep several women
Are a drain on the Lama's wealth –
Avoid it by placing their quarters apart.
Pilfering the communal kitchen
Augurs rebirth in hell –
Avert it by moderating desire.
Errantly falling asleep in assembly
Augers rebirth as a beast –
Avert it by sweeping out laziness.
Excessive reverence for women
Is the bane of doting elders –
Destroy it by maintaining self-control.
Loaning money for profit
Is a danger to monks following the Teaching –
Avert it by tempering needs, content in simple experience.
Preaching the Law with pride and vanity

Is the weakness of scholars and teachers –
Remove it through humility and tranquility.
The sweet smiles of nuns
Are the plague of Gomchens –
Avoid it through self-control.
Attachment to fashionable jewelry
Is the bane of all women –
Destroy it by dressing them in patched rags.
The Lama's thick penis
Is the plague of nuns –
Avoid it by shouting to awaken the neighbours.
The birth of bastards
Is the fate of whores –
Avert it by showing them the door.
Hoarding wealth
Is the failing of the rich –
Avoid it by sponsoring monastic rites.
Hubris in a general
Augurs battles lost –
Avert this through faith in a reliable war-god.
Cutting stone and digging foundations of a castle
Portend the end of a family line –[10]
Avert it by powerful protective rites.
Mother's long fingernails
Spell disaster to father's balls –
Avert it by cutting her nails with a small sharp knife.
A stick of mother's stack of firewood
Is a danger in father's hand –
Avert it by snatching and burning it.
Taking refuge in silence with upraised eyes
Stirs father's wrath –
Avert this with long suffering patience.
Borrowing countless loans
Is the plague of the starving poor –
Avert it by taking service with the rich.
An alcoholic father
Is a disaster for the whole family –
He should avert it by controlling his mind.
Coughing and erection of the penis
Disturb one's own and other's sleep –
Avert this by eating garlic and capsicum.
Brigands and robbers
Portend disaster to the rich –

Avert it by liberal spending.
Disloyal monks without commitment
Cause trouble in the monastery –
Avert it by expelling the mischief makers.
Gifts of small patches of land to the monastery
Forbode friction between the donors and recipients –
Avert it by sustaining good friendship.
Sour and rotten chung
Is a disaster for the stomach and intestines –
Avert it by drinking hot, medicinal soup.
A garrulous gossiping woman
Is a plague on the neighbours –
Avert it by refusing to converse.
At midnight when father sighs
And mother moans,
When the clever child awakes
And begins to giggle,
When the baby cries from its cot,
Father's organ is penetrating mother –
Give the children nuts to eat!
Each glass of chung demands a pee,
And restraining it, it leaks on the doorstep;
Pressing your organ, your nose begins to run,
And full to the brim, you cough and splutter
Until the spitoon becomes full;
The filth offends the Serpents[11]
And the family is afflicted with colds,
With tumors and abscesses to follow –
Avoid them by cleanliness and burning incense!
Kneading dough without washing hands,
Absorbed in the work, the soup boils over;
The soup burns, and stinks in the fire,
And the room is filled with flying ash;
The eyes of the guests fill with tears from the smoke
And the children wail with hunger;
Father cannot cope with the problem
And mother is faced with disaster –
She averts this by rising earlier for breakfast!'

All the people who were watching the Lama were awe struck. A couple of ignorant, indolent people had this sort of thing to say: 'What is this idiot madman saying? There is no such liturgy! He is talking rubbish!' But another faction who had some intelligence and seemed to be spiritual counsellors prostrated to him. 'Drukpa Kunley's Liturgy of Protection from Disaster seems to be lay conceit,' they advised, 'but it is actually teaching upon non-attachment to whatever arises in the stream of consciousness.' And they took refuge in him. Those who folded their hands in reverence were filled with faith.

Transporting himself to Lhasa in an instant, in order to show his manifold powers of magic, the Master of Truth, Lord of Beings, Kunga Legpa, encountered a band of Kongpo merchants carrying loads of spears. 'Please give me a spear!' he demanded of their leader.

'I'll give it to you all right,' said the merchant, pressing the spear into the Lama's breast. 'I risked my life getting these spears. Why should I give them away?'

'Let's see if your spear of ignorance is as powerful as my spear of Empty and Pure Awareness!' said the Lama. And he grabbed the head of the spear that was thrust at him, pulling it like elastic and tying a knot in it.

'You must be a ghost or a demon or a great Adept,' said the frightened leader. 'Tell us who you are.'

'I'm whoever you think I am,' replied Kunley. 'It makes no difference to me.'

'You must be an Adept,' said another merchant. 'Forgive us for offending you by suggesting that you are a ghost or demon. Here, take this whole load of spears for the one you have knotted!'

Kunley gave him the spear and vanished.

It is said that a chieftain of Kham gave twenty-one villages for this spear.

It was at this time that the Rinpung Chieftain sent an invitation to the Lama to visit Rinpung[12] with the intention of testing his powers. The Lama accepted the invitation, and arriving at the gate of the Chieftain's castle, he was greeted by an official who asked him to wait outside while he chained the dogs. Kunley did not heed him and went inside immediately, only to be set upon by two dogs, one a giant white mastiff and the other a giant black mastiff. He raised his staff and struck them both on their backs, severing their fore quarters from their hind quarters. 'What is the use of all black and all white dogs?' he commented, joining a black part to a white part and vice versa. He then restored the dogs without a trace of injury, and they began to frolic around the courtyard like puppies.

Many people gathered together in curiosity. 'Rather than stand around in idle curiosity watching my magic tricks and listening to my insane raving, it would be better for you to recite the MANI PEME Mantra,' he said, and began to perform the Mani Dance called Exhortation to Continuous Awareness of Impermanence, singing this song:

'Ho! Listen to me you men and gods!
All those who have achieved a human body
And can say, 'I always keep my next death in mind',
They will find the Sacred Path of Buddhas.
And he who can say, 'The Sacred Teaching has manifest',
He can turn and revere Samsara.

'Gazing into the vault of the mid-day sky
Look at the hundreds of large birds and thousands of small birds
And realize that no matter how high they fly
They are all bound for the City of Death.
Certain that we all must die,
Anxious, ignorant of the time and place,
We should take refuge in the Great Compassionate One
And recite his Six Syllable Mantra:
OM MANI PEME HUNG![13]

'Gaze down into the depths of the river below
And look at the hundreds of large fish and thousands of small fish
And realize that all of those golden-eyed fishes
Are swimming towards the City of Death.
Certain that we all must die,
Anxious, ignorant of the time and place,
We should take refuge in the Great Compassionate One[14]
And recite his Six Syllable Mantra:
OM MANI PEME HUNG!

'Gazing around you in this world of limbo
Look at mankind and the four-footed beasts of the Four
    Continents

And realize that all who draw breath,
Uncertain which of the young or old will be first to die,
All hasten towards the City of Death.
Certain that we all must die,
Anxious, ignorant of the time and place,
We should take refuge in the Great Compassionate One
And recite his Six Syllable Mantra:
OM MANI PEME HUNG!'

Dancing and singing, the Lama exhorted the Chieftain and his officials to arise and join the dance. They gained great faith, and felt profound aversion to temporal attachments. The Chieftain offered him the key to his treasure house, insisting that he should help himself to the treasure. Opening the door the Lama found gold bars stacked on one side, silver ingots stacked on the other side, and ornaments encrusted with jewels lying everywhere in heaps. He dressed himself in silver, gold and jewels, and tying a white silk sash around his waist he went outside to display himself to the people. Then he took off his finery and returned it to the Chieftain, who, however, insisted that he should keep it.

'You can't take it with you!' said the Lama. 'A moment of enjoyment is sufficient. Listen to my song!'

'Bathe us in bliss-waves, Father Kahgyu Lama![15]
Gold, silver and jewels are illusory happiness
While losing wealth is illusory sadness –
Take refuge in the man without wealth or possessions!

'A beautiful lifelong companion is illusory happiness
And parting of lovers is seemingly sad –
Take refuge in the friendless and family-free!

'Incarnation in a precious human body is illusory happiness
And leaving it empty-handed is seemingly sad –
Take refuge in the heart of the human situation!

'Fulfilment of ambition for wealth and status is illusory
    happiness
And seeing it snatched away by others is seemingly sad –
Take refuge in the man who is infinitely generous!

'Gaining the goal of one's life is illusory happiness

And the parting of body and mind at death is seemingly sad –
Take refuge in striving for everlasting bliss!'

At the end of his song his audience was burning with faith
and devotion. 'Lord of Naljorpas! Obviously you are satisfied merely by the gifts your sense fields provide. But please
accept this fine quality grain.'

The Lama accepted the grain and left the Chieftain's
house to find a chung house in the nearest village. The
mother and daughter who owned the chung house mistook
him for a drunken Kongpo monk and offered to serve him
liquor in exchange for a song. So he sang them this song:

'What everyone needs is Nirvana;[16]
What one needs for oneself is independence;
What the worldly man needs is wealth;
What young girls need is a donkey's penis;
What old ladies need is malicious gossip;
And what old age needs is many sons.
To give freely is generosity;
To be free from avarice is wealth.
I am the Duty-Free Kunga Legpa
And you two, mother and daughter,
Are my generous patrons!'

They served him as much chung as he could drink, until,
finally, he sang this song to the people:

'The hill is covered with forest
Yet firewood in the home is scarce;
The wide river is flowing below
Yet water for chung is scarce;
The town is full of barley
But a free glass of chung is scarce;
The market is full of girls
But desirable pussy is scarce;
The Tradition has spread throughout the land
But Wisdom and Knowledge are scarce.'

Finishing his song, he left that village.

'It's time for Palzang Buti!' thought the Lama to himself,
and he set off for Lhasa. On the way he met some young
girls singing this song:

'In the middle of U, in Central Tibet,
Lies the Religious Centre of Lhasa,
Where all the Omniscient Buddhas sit
Turning the Wheel of the Law.'

'I will dance now,' said the Lama, 'and you must follow my movements!' and he sang this:

'In the cleansing, cleansing spring,
Sword sways, sways to and fro,
Rocks rub, rub together,
Head rises, rises proudly,
Now tightly grasp it, grasp it tightly!'

'We don't mix with people like you!' said the girls.

'Yah! Yah!' replied the Lama. 'If we don't get along there's no point in my staying!' And he continued on his way to Palzang Buti's house.

He found her standing at the door. 'Last year, an old man of Lhasa told me about a Palzang Buti. You must be she!' he said.

'Yes, I'm Palzang Buti. Come inside.' She felt him to be an old friend from a previous life and accepted him without constraint. Before serving him tea they made love. Afterwards she begged him to stay with her for ever, but he promised her only a few months.

One day he visited the monastery of Drepung.[17] Sitting with the monks he thought he should play a joke on the Moral Guard.[18]

'I would like to become a novice,' he told them.

'Where do you come from?' he was asked.

'I am a Drukpa,' he said.

'Do the Drukpas have good voices?'

'I don't have such a good voice,' he told them innocently, 'but I have a friend who is an excellent chanter.'

'Bring your friend with you tomorrow,' they told him.

The next day when the monks had assembled, the Lama brought a donkey by the ear, covered him with a red robe, and sat him down at the end of the line of monks.

'What is this!' exclaimed the Moral Guard in wrath.

'This is my friend with the good voice,' Kunley told

them, kicking the donkey to make it bray. The Guard chased him away with sticks, with the Lama shouting over his shoulder to them, 'You people care more about chanting than meditation!'

While returning to Lhasa, two monks from the assembly caught up with him and asked him where he was bound.

'Drukpa Kunley has no home and no destination,' he replied. 'I have no place at Drepung and no place in hell.'

'What crime did you commit that hell wasn't deep enough for you?' they asked, laughing.

'In this human world,' said the Lama, 'I did whatever came into my mind, but I came into conflict with other men's desires, so I thought that I should spend a couple of days in hell. But the road was blocked by monks from Sera Monastery.[19] Then I returned and decided to become a monk at Drepung, but the monastery was filled with Jealousy, Lust, and Anger, and I could find no place.' And so saying, he returned to Lhasa.

At Palzang Buti's house he would drink strong chung and keep his stomach contented until mid-day; then from mid-day to nightfall he would play and sing either to the lute or flute; from sunset to midnight he would make love to Palzang Buti; and from midnight to dawn he sat cultivating his Mahamudra perspective.[20]

One day the Lama thought to himself that it was wrong to have been so long in Lhasa without meeting a Buddha Lama, and he determined to visit the Buddha Tsongkhapa.[21] 'It is said that Tsongkhapa is an incarnation of the Bodhisattva of Intelligence,'[22] Drukpa Kunley told Palzang Buti. 'I must see if his mind is free of lust and anger.'

At the temple of Ramoche,[23] he found the monks engaged in metaphysical discussion, and thinking that he should not lose this opportunity to teach them how to laugh, he asked, 'What are you doing, O monks?'

'We are cleansing our spiritual perspective of doubts and disharmonies,' they told him. 'I know a little bit of metaphysics myself,' said the Lama, grabbing a handful of his own flatulence and thrusting it under their noses. 'Which came first, the air or the smell?' he demanded.

'This is my friend with the good voice. . . .'

The monks became angry and would chase him away. 'We are not fitting butts for your humour!' they abused him.

'Don't be so proud,' the Lama responded. 'Relax a little. My ways and your ways are somewhat different. My ways are civilized while your ways are full of lust and pride. Now would you please announce me to the Bodhisattva of Intelligence, Tsongkhapa.'

'Where is your formal offering?' they asked him.

'I didn't know I should need one,' the Lama remonstrated. 'I'll bring one next time I come. I must see him today.'

'Whoever heard of bringing an offering later!' the monks scoffed.

'If it's absolutely necessary,' offered the Lama finally, 'I have this fine pair of testicles given to me by my parents, will they do?'

The monks became angry again, and denying him entry, chased him away.

'When I have found an offering I will return to plague these monks,' thought the Lama, and made his way back to Lhasa.

The following day he told Palzang Buti that he was going to Samye to find an offering for Tsongkhapa.

Returning to Samye he went to the house of the local government official called Pebdak, where he was greeted respectfully by husband and wife. 'Welcome, Precious Master of Truth!' said Pebdak. 'Since you performed the rites of Vow Reparation and Destruction of Evil Forces at the Samye Dodechopa, we have had good luck and an abundant harvest. When I was in Zilung in China last year, I met a Kongpo trader who told me how a Lama had knotted a spear through his magical power. Since then I have been longing to meet you again. I am honoured to have you here today.' And Pebdak offered the Lama food and chung with the very best of service.

Later Pebdak asked for the Lama's help. 'I have had three wives of whom two died shortly after I married them. My present wife has given birth to six sons, but none of them has lived longer than three months. This year my wife gave birth to another son who is now nearly three months old. I entreat your blessings upon him, and beg you to perform a rite that will keep all destructive forces out of him.'

'What is your son's name?' asked the Lama. 'Bring him here.'

'His name is Samye Guardian,' Pebdak told him. 'He was born healthy and intelligent.'

When Pebdak's wife brought her son, the child immediately began to shake and tremble. 'Stay still! Don't be afraid!' the Lama commanded, and he asked Pebdak to bring a black lassoo that he had seen hanging upon a pillar. He put the noose round the child's neck as it lay in its mother's lap and said, 'If you don't lick my cock today, my name isn't Drukpa Kunley! Now down to the river!' Dragging the child behind him with the lassoo, followed by the parents wailing, swallowing dust, chewing stones, and tearing their hair, he reached the river bank. 'If you dare to return here again, you'll get this same treatment,' said the Lama holding the child at arm's length by the neck and then hurling him into the centre of the swirling stream. Suddenly the child's corpse was seen to change into a black dog with a gaping red mouth which snarled, 'You've no compassion, Drukpa Kunley!' as it swam to the opposite bank.

'That was your son!' he told the parents, and gaining complete faith in the Lama, they returned to their house blameless and free from fear.

Back in Pebdak's house the Lama taught this method of Destroying Evil Influences that might threaten their children:

'The baby crying in its cradle at midnight,
Signifies father's penetration of his wife –
Calm the baby by giving it nuts to eat.
If this device is ineffective
Wrap his head in bed clothes in a corner.
Possession of the child by an angry demon[24]
Portends endless human misery –
Avert it with the Lama's protecting charm.
If the charm is ineffective

Destroy the demon by a Rite of Exorcism.
A useless and impotent son
Portends the end of the family line –
I, Drukpa Kunley, can remove that curse.
And if my blessing is ineffective,
A noose around his neck will destroy the bane.'

After giving this teaching, the Lama told Pebdak and his wife that they should expect another son by the same time next year.

'Please name the child now,' Pebdak requested. 'You may not be here next year.'

'Call him Abundant Harvest, because he will be the origin of a flourishing line,' said the Lama.

When Pebdak's wife heard this prediction, she offered the Lama her jewelry as a token of her gratitude, and Pebdak himself presented the Lama with a box of fifty gold coins and a turquoise. The Lama decked himself with the Lady's ornaments and then returned them to her saying that wearing them for an instant was quite enough. He returned the gold and turquoise also, but Pebdak insisted that he keep them in order to bring good fortune upon his family and to remove any obstacles that would arise in his path. The Lama finally accepted the gifts with the avowed intention of offering them to Tsongkhapa. He put the turquoise into the aperture of his Thunderbolt,[25] took the gold in his hand, and left Samye for Lhasa.

In the market place at Lhasa all eyes boggled at his treasure. 'If you want gold, pay with turquoise. If you want turquoise, pay in gold!' he shouted.

'You'll find no buyer for so much gold,' he was told. 'And the turquoise is stuck in a strictly sacred place, so no one will want it.' But interested to see what the Lama would do with it, a crowd followed him. He went straight to the Temple of the Glorious Goddess, where he found seven girls dancing and singing the praises of the goddess:

'Enshrined in this golden pagoda
Protectress, Only Mother, Glorious Goddess,[26]
Possessor of the Eye of Wisdom,
To you we girls sing praises!'

'You sing very sweetly,' the Lama told them. 'Now listen to me.'

'In this Religious Centre of Holy Lhasa
Incense and butter lamps are the customary offerings
To our Only Mother, the Glorious Goddess;
But today, Duty-Free Kunga Legpa
Offers his penis and his turquoise.
Accept it, Goddess, and show us compassion!'

Then he threw the turquoise to the Goddess. Today the stone can still be seen in her forehead.

Leaving the temple he set off to visit the Bodhisattva of Intelligence, Tsongkhapa. As soon as he arrived at the Ramoche Temple, the monks asked him what he was doing there.

'I've come for audience with the Buddha Tsongkhapa,' he told them.

'Do you still only have your balls as offerings?' jibed the monks.

'No. This time I have gold to offer him,' responded the Lama.

'Then you can gain audience immediately.'

'Yah! Yah!' laughed the Lama. 'If one has gold to offer, the way is immediately opened.' And he thought to himself that he should open these monks' eyes for them.

Ushered into the Presence, he proceeded to prostrate to the box of gold intoning these words:

'I bow to the Illuminator of our Darkness,
The Crown of Tibetan Sages, Tsongkhapa!
I bow to the inviolate Keeper of the Three Vows,
Bearer of the White Lotus who was prophesied by Atisha![27]
I bow to teacher, debater and composer,
Bearer of the Sword on the Utpala Lotus![28]
I bow to the saviour of the poor, he who relieves poverty,
Possessor of divine charisma, covered by a web of gold!
I bow to the lover of wealth and comfort –
May this offering of gold bring joy to his heart!
I bow to him whose eyes turned from a poor and lowly votary
When I visited you last year with no offering!'

'O Lord of Beings, Kunga Legpa, you speak truthfully

and it is good to hear you,' Tsongkhapa said in reply. He knotted a protective thread[29] and gave it to the Lama, asking him to accept it as a blessing. 'You need nothing more than this,' he said. 'Wear it!'

The Lama accepted the token and withdrew. 'What shall I do with this thread?' he thought to himself. 'It is not comfortable to wear around my neck. I have no pocket to put it into, and I don't want to carry it in my hand. Better I tie it around my penis which is quite clean and has nothing to carry.' So he wrapped it around his penis and went to the market.

'Look! Look!' he shouted. 'If you have fifty pieces of gold you can gain audience with the Buddha Tsongkhapa himself. He may even give you one of these!' And he waved his member with the thread around it in the air.

Now in the market at Lhasa, lived an innkeeper, who was named Lhadron. She was a notorious thief, tricking traders out of their goods and their money. A Yamdrok trader was staying there at that time, and his hostess was intending to replace his amber with some imitations. The Lama was aware of this and went to the inn for a drink in the chung parlour.

'Everybody is happy here,' he said. 'The hostess must be an excellent woman! And since everybody's tongue is loose, the chung must be first class. There's an old saying, "Good chung is good for the health, and good stories are good for the mind." If you give me some quality chung, I will tell you a first class story.'

'Tell us your story!' said the innkeeper.

Once upon a time, in the upper part of a valley called Nangyul, lived a trickster called Lying Greed and his two sons, Duwa and Duchung. In the valley below lived a poor man called Faint Heart. These two were companions in their constant search for sustenance. One day in their travels from valley to valley they were resting beneath a tree when they noticed that the tree seemed to glitter. Realising that the source of the glow was underground, they dug down and found a pot of gold. This discovery sent them into rapture.

Finally, Faint Heart said:

'Listen Lying Greed, my friend of many lifetimes!
Our past affinities have joined us in friendship
Yet the fruit of our virtue has been hoarded
And avarice has caused us poverty.
But in so far as we have been poor and generous
Today we reap the harvest of our liberality –
Today we have found a treasure trove.
We should make of it an offering to the Buddhas.
Is that not right? Consider this carefully.'

'Today through a coincidence of virtue and luck, we have found this treasure,' Lying Greed opined. 'And since it is your merit more than mine that has caused this good fortune, I shall give a three day feast of chung and meat in your honour. Just now I will take the gold and divide it fairly into two parts. But beware! good friend. This gold could be an illusion, a trick of gods or demons.'

'That is highly unlikely,' Faint Heart said sceptically. 'But if it is an illusion, there is little that we can do about it.'

Faint Heart went home. But Lying Greed took the gold, hid it in the ground in a secret place, and refilled the pot with sawdust. When Faint Heart returned, he found Lying Greed crying under the tree.

'What is the matter, friend?' he asked.

'I told you that the gold could be an illusion, and so it turned out,' Lying Greed moaned.

'You must be lying,' said Faint Heart. 'I never heard of such a thing before. But even if it is true, there's nothing to cry about.'

Lying Greed plied his friend with chung, and commanded his boys to dance for him.

'Friend, your sons dance like phantoms or figments of a dream,' Faint Heart commented. 'It certainly makes a fine spectacle.'

Some time later Faint Heart visited Lying Greed with a barrel of chung, and they ate and drank and made merry. When they were both intoxicated, Faint Heart suggested that his friend send his sons to stay with him and his wife down in the valley, saying that it would please the doting woman, and give her pleasure to see them sing and dance. Faint Heart asked his friend to come himself after three days, and again they would drink and feast. Forgetting his guilt and the grudge that his friend bore him, Lying Greed acquiesced.

Now Faint Heart had two monkeys which he had trained to obey him, and when Lying Greed came to visit him after the three days had passed, he found his friend weeping.

'What's the matter?' he asked.

'Your two sons have turned into monkeys,' Faint Heart moaned. 'You remember when they were dancing at your house last week I said that they looked like phantoms? Well it seems that I was right!'

'I never heard of boys changing into monkeys,' said Lying Greed in scorn. 'Please return my sons to me at once.'

Faint Heart replied:

> 'Lying Greed, my friend, please listen to me!
> We two have been friends long since
> And we have seen strange things together.
> We saw gold dust turn into sawdust –
> Something that has never been seen before.
> And now your boys have turned into monkeys.
> These calamities that have befallen us
> Are unprecedented and senseless omens.
> If you doubt that these monkeys are your sons –
> Look! "Go to your father, you monkeys!" '

And the monkeys ran and sat in Lying Greed's lap.

'What has become of my sons?' he wailed. 'This must be divine retribution for exchanging the gold dust for sawdust. But I confess! I will bring the gold dust to you. Now please give me back my two sons.'

'Bring the gold dust first,' Faint Heart told him. 'Then I may do something for you.'

Lying Greed retrieved the gold dust, divided it into two, gave Faint Heart his portion, and regained his sons.

Now when these two men died, they were brought before the court of the Lord of Death to be rewarded and punished for their good and bad deeds. The result of Lying Greed's deception was incarceration in the burning iron house in hell. For tricking Lying Greed, Faint Heart was sentenced to twelve years' rebirth as a monkey.

The Lama finished his story, and the innkeeper abandoned her intention to steel the merchant's amber. The merchant was thus saved from financial disaster, and their hostess was saved from rebirth in hell.

3 How Drukpa Kunley visited Taklung, Yalpachen, and Sakya, to give Meaning to the Lives of the People

We bow at the feet of Kunga Legpa, the Great Adept,
Who through the karma of his impartial, spontaneous, ascetic activity,
Revealed strange miracles and truth
Precisely in accord with his every intention.

Then the Lord of Beings, Master of Truth, Kunga Legpa himself, travelled north to Taklung Monastery,[1] where he encountered the Taklung Rimpoche. 'I have heard that you are well-versed in the Sutras and Tantras, and that you have a particular genius for stripping reality to the bone, revealing your own faults and the defects of others,' said Taklung Rimpoche. 'Sing me a really pleasant song that shows me imperfection and excellence. Here is my lute to accompany yourself with.'

So the Lama sang this song:

'Look at the distress of donkeys carrying their intolerable burdens
And then look at the ecstasy of the stallion, galloping wild and free.
Look at the misery of hoopoe birds strutting about ruined houses
Then look at the exhilaration of the eagle, knifing through the sky.
Look at the sadness of miserable mice with flip-flopping ears
Then look at the joy of the fish darting through the water.
Look at the hardships of horse-riding, spear-carrying barbarians
Then look at the bliss of the Sage,[2] perceiving the Emptiness of illusion.
Look at the frustration of the wet arses of the Dezhol girls
And then look at the tight sheaths of the nuns in their mountain caves.
Look at the amount of lewd desire in the Taklung Mountain Hermitage

And then look at the formidable vows of guilt and shame.
Look at the intensity of the Tulku's[3] perception, grasping
  other men's minds
And then look at Kunley's joy in total renunciation.'

The Incarnate Buddha was impressed. 'You are truly
wise in both mundane and divine wisdom,' he said. 'There
is really nothing more to say. Steward! Bring me what you
have in your hand.' And the steward, who was wearing
improper casual dress, brought a shapely pastry elephant
into which the Rimpoche stuck a stick of white incense.
'Sing us a song in praise of this gift I'm giving you,' he
requested. And Drukpa Kunley sang this song:

> 'In a temple without a pagoda roof
> And walls without frescos
> Reclines a Lama without generosity.
> I, Drukpa Kunley, without any reputation as dung monger,
> Sing this song of praise without rhyme
> To the elephant without consciousness
> Implanted with incense without scent
> Offered me by a steward without vow!'

The onlookers giggled, while the Incarnation was induced to offer the Lama his best hospitality. It was at this
time that the Lama took Taklung Ngawong Drakpa's
daughter as his consort.[4] After performing many miracles
and delivering a wondrous stream of teaching, he disappeared.

The Lama continued on his pilgrimage to Yalpachen. Here
he found the Karmapa,[5] who was wearing his Black Hat,
enthroned under a canopy, and giving instruction to a vast
concourse of people assembled in the market place. In the
crowd was a strikingly beautiful girl called Mistress Palzang. The Lama layed a stick over his shoulder and walked
around the market place all the time shouting, 'Karmapa has
broken his Vow!'

Some monks took sticks to beat him but Karmapa inter-
vened, 'Don't beat him! Don't beat him! He is quite right,'
he called. 'This man has the power to read other people's
minds. He is the reincarnation of the Indian Adept Shava-

ripa. The truth is that, just as all men are attracted by beautiful women, myself being no exception, setting my eyes upon that fascinating girl over there I was possessed by her beauty for a moment, although I had no real lust for her. Drukpa Kunley was aware of this, and he was quite right in his accusation. Sing us a song of the situation, Naljorpa!'

And Kunley sang:

> 'This girl is like the devil's daughter,
> For although she carries no hook or noose,[6]
> Merely by a flash of her eye
> She can summon and bind a man's mind –
> She can even turn a Buddha's mind!
> Charming, radiant, sweet-voiced maiden,
> Whispering fondly and intimately
> You give ephemeral joy that curdles!
> Your beautiful body, face fair and flushed,
> Your seductive fickle talking,
> Drowns one helplessly in Samsara.
> Desire not! Resist attraction, Karmapa!
>
> 'But the youthful Indian peacock
> Makes its seat a cushion of thorn
> Where other creatures dare not sit.
> And the elegant Tibetan cock
> Eats poisonous seeds to sate its hunger –
> Food fatal to other creatures.
> I, Drukpa Kunley of Ralung,
> Can think thoughts of beautiful women
> That are perilous to you, the Lord Karmapa.'

'Who gave you permission to do what is prohibited to others?' demanded a monk.

'There is a paradise called Ogmin,'[7] replied the Lama, 'where no ordinary man can go. And in the middle of that vast paradise is a marvellous palace where the scintillating blue Vajra Bearer lives. Through Tilopa and Naropa[8] he relayed instruction to me informing me what I can and what I cannot do.' The crowd was satisfied by this disclosure and became subdued in devotion.

'In the discipline of mind-training,' the Karmapa smiled, 'I am your superior. But in realization of the identical, pure nature of all things, you are my peer. In the future, people will remember your name before mine.'

Some people say that the Karmapa then took the Naljorpa with him to his Tsurphu monastery. If this is so, then that Karmapa was Mikyo Dorje (1507-54). The story relates how the Lama examined the Karmapa's Mahamudra realization, and how he wished to propagate the Mahamudra doctrine at Tolung Tsurphu, but finding only lecherous monks and ill-omens at the monastery, he sang the Song of the Nine Bad Omens and left:

'In this monastery of yours with a black mountain behind, a black lake in front, a black roof on the palace, a black, dark assembly room, black-dog monks, a black faced steward, a black hatted Lama, a black Reality Protector,[9] and women with black beavers, in this place of the Nine Black Omens I will not stay.'

Then the Master of Truth, Lord of Beings, Drukpa Kunley, decided to examine the realization of Sakya Panchen.[10] He journeyed to Sakya and found himself at the Temple of Loving Kindness, where the monks were celebrating the annual Rite of Mourning for the Incarnation of Loving Kindness.[11] The Lama saw immediately that the Incarnation had been reborn as a donkey which at that moment was struggling up the hill with an immense burden upon its back. The Lama asked the donkey's master to lend him the animal, which he then led back by the ear to the temple.

'What is that?' asked the monks.

'As you can see, it's a donkey,' replied the Lama. 'And what are you all doing?'

'Today we perform the ritual offering for the return of our deceased Lama,' they told him.

'What is his name?' the Lama wanted to know.

'The Tulku of Loving Kindness,' they told him.

'And where is he now?' the Lama continued questioning.

'In the Galden Paradise,'[12] they replied.

'And where is that?'

'It is very difficult to find,' they responded vaguely. 'Don't ask so many questions.' Folding their hands in prayer, closing their eyes, they ignored him, and proceeded to offer this intercession to their Rimpoche:

> 'Bodhisattva of Intelligence, seeing identity in
> universal simplicity!
> Great Diamond Being, endowed with the Fivefold
> Perfection of Awareness![13]
> Incarnation of Loving Kindness! we pray to you
> To sustain us with your ambrosial blessings,
> And to bestow upon us power and realization.'

The Lama offered a prayer to the donkey:

> 'Donkey, most pitiful of beasts!
> Rarely finding grass or water,
> Overloaded, overburdened,
> We pray to your beaten backside
> For the blessings of your bent shoulder.'

The Lamas were outraged. 'Pray to our Lama, not the donkey!' they shouted.

'Your Lama was reborn as this donkey,' the Lama informed them.

'What nonsense!' they told him.

'When your Lama was travelling through Tibet, China and Mongolia,' the Lama hastened to explain, 'he overloaded his pack horses, and the result of that karma was rebirth as a donkey.' And as if to verify this, the donkey's eyes filled with tears.

Seeing this, convinced of Kunley's story, the monks folded their hands in reverence to the donkey and asked the Lama when their Lama would return to govern the monastery.

'If you want your Lama to return quickly,' he told them, 'feed the donkey kindly for five years, and when it dies the Lama will be reborn in Lithang in Kham and then return to you here.'

They did as the Lama advised, and, indeed, their Rimpoche, the Incarnation of Loving Kindness, was reborn in Lithang and returned eventually to Sakya.

Then having passed through the town of Serdokchen (near Sakya), the Lama was sunning his backside on a rock when Sakya Panchen himself appeared with a hundred servants.

'Get up, Drukpa Kunley!' he called. 'Don't be so crass!'
The Lama replied to him in verse:

'Never knowing any physical discomfort,
Hoping for Buddhahood in coloured robes,
Sending your disciples to hell,
I feel sad to set eyes upon you.
Be on your way, Sakya Panchen, Lord of Beings!
Go! Give your discourses and initiations,
Gather around you your vow violators,
Sow your seeds of disaster,
Cultivate your plants of delusion,
Grow your shoots of passion,
Ripen your karma of the Bardo,
Carry the sins of old women,
Fulfil your duty to your dependents,
And fill your treasure houses with riches!'

Sakya Panchen smiled and replied with these verses:

'Here by a cave without door or pillar,
Sits Drukpa Kunley with the dirty mouth
Who babbles nonsense wherever he is.
I feel great pity for you!
Go! Wander the world without purpose,
Destroy the faith of the people you meet,
Carry your wealth on your penis head,
Offer your sacred substance to whores,
Arouse the dogs with your door-knocking
And break the ribs of the eldest bitches;
Pick your nits and toss them like stones behind you,
Break the hip bones of your women,
And sun-bathe wherever you wish!'

Feeling pleased with their verses and their mutual understanding, Sakya Panchen invited the Lama to his monastery, giving him a horse to ride. On the road they passed some Tsawa Rongpa girls working in the fields. They began to tease the monks.

'You want to jig-jig?' they called.

'No one feels like making out today,' shouted the Lama from the head of the procession.

'Don't speak like that in front of the monks,' Sakya Panchen whispered angrily.

'What's the matter?' Kunley asked innocently. 'All girls like to get laid.'

Sakya Panchen spurred his horse on ahead in disgust.

After they had reached Sakya, the Panchen showed Drukpa Kunley a magic word square in which every line began with the letter NGA (I) and was written in self-adulation.

'See if you can do as well!' challenged Sakya Panchen.

'I cannot ridicule you, such an exalted descendant of the Kon race,[14] and I don't know the art of eulogy so I shall simply add a letter U to your NGA.' So instead of

> 'I, Sakya Panchen of To,
> I, Ruler of the Chinese Plains,
> I, Master of the Snowland Valleys,
> I, the Diadem of all living beings, etc.'

we have:

> 'The Sakya Panchen of To is weeping,
> The Ruler of the Chinese Plains is weeping,
> The Master of the Snowland Valleys is weeping,
> The Diadem of all living beings is weeping, etc.'

The Panchen laughed, enjoying the thrust at himself, and then suggested a competition in letters for their mutual enjoyment. He wrote the MANI PEME Mantra in Lantsa script[15] and showed it to the Lama. Drukpa Kunley was unimpressed and proceeded to give a demonstration of his own. 'When I bend my elbows and put my hands to the height of my shoulders, I form the letter A; when I place my hands in meditation mudra, I form the letter CHA; when I raise my left leg to my crotch and stand upon my right foot like this, I form the letter NA.' In this way he demonstrated the whole of the Tibetan alphabet.

Later, when they were eating, Sakya Panchen tested the Lama again. Taking a piece of dough he pulled it into the shape of a deer and showed it to Kunley. 'If you have any skill in your hands, spontaneously create an animal like this,' he suggested.

Pulling the dough and cutting it without any hesitation, Kunley showed them a snake and a dragon. His audience was impressed.

'He is a good magician,' thought Sakya Panchen. 'I should show his magic to the Chinese.' And to the Lama he said, 'In the future to be sure that our two lineages will blend in harmony, we should make a short trip to China together.'

They set off immediately. On the way the Lama relieved the Panchen and his attendants' boredom with games and magical display.

When they reached the Emperor of China's palace, Drukpa Kunley pretended to be a messenger and sat at the end of the line of the Panchen's attendants in the meanest position. When they took their meal of roast carcasses of mutton, Kunley found only a meatless carcass of bone and gristle at the bottom of the wooden basket. He sang this song in disgust:

> 'Sakya Panchen of To
> Has needs the same as his servants,
> But the distribution of the meat is unfair –
> Some receive good meat and some receive bad.
> All sheep, it is true, are mutton
> But some are fat and some are thin.
> What were you doing, O sheep,
> When your friends were grazing and drinking?
> You only become fat by grazing –
> Now go back to the fields to eat!'

The Lama slapped the sheep's carcass, whereupon it stood up and bounded out of the door to run back to the mountains.

'If the servant can do such tricks,' said the Chinese in astonishment, 'what can we expect from the Master?' Sakya Panchen had been to China three times before, but never did he receive such rich offerings and adulation.

After they had returned to Sakya, the Lama stayed for a few days in the neighbourhood of an extremely beautiful lady called Loleg Buti. The Lama wanted to ride her but she refused his advances. He was abashed. 'How can there be such a woman!' he stormed, and stamped his foot on a flat stone, impressing his footprint in it as if it were mud. This exploit was noised about throughout the area, and Loleg

Buti repented her hastiness and brought first class chung to the Lama as an offering.

'O Great Adept!' she said. 'The first time I met you I didn't recognize that you were a Buddha. Please forgive me and take my body now.'

'Raise your skirt and open your legs,' ordered the Lama.

'A kha kha!' said the Lama, looking between her thighs and taking out his organ, 'It seems that we are not suited to one another. You need a triangular organ, and I need a round aperture. Obviously we can't do business!'

The girl suddenly became sick of the world. 'O Precious Master of Truth!' she entreated him. 'If you think me a superior woman please take me with you; if you think that I'm a mediocrity, send me to a hermitage; and if you think I'm an inferior person cut my hair and give me a religious name.'

'You are not a woman I can take with me,' the Lama replied. 'And you are unfit for a hermitage, so it must be your third option. What name do you want?'

'Give me a common name,' she requested.

'Earth Water Fire Air Sky Saviouress,' he offered.

'I don't want a name like that,' she said. 'I want a musical name.'

'Vina Flute Lute Saviouress,' he named her.

'That will make me shy,' she said. 'Give me a terrific name.'

'Then you shall be Leopard Bear Serpent Saviouress.'

'No! It is better that I have a soft name,' she responded.

'Silk Brocade Medicine Saviouress.'

'Lama, please stop teasing me,' she pleaded. 'Please give me a name to my taste.'

'Molasses Sugar Honey Saviouress.'

'No name like that,' she protested. 'I am sick of the world, and I have decided to devote my life to Religion. Please give me a suitable name that shows that I have taken refuge in Buddha.'

'Disgusted Devout Refuge Saviouress.'

'Still I'm not satisfied!'

'Then we'll call you Lustful Shameless Divine-Teaching Saviouress,' he suggested.

'Leave out the first two words and let me have the rest,

Divine-Teaching Saviouress (Lhacho Drolma),' she begged. And the Lama complied.

He sent her to meditate on Jomo Lhari,[16] instructing her to stay there for three years. During those three years she ate nothing, sustaining herself on the nourishment of deep concentration, always keeping her eyes open. Finally, by the grace of the Lama, Lhacho Drolma achieved Buddhahood in a Body of Light.

Amongst the Lama's five thousand girl friends, thirteen were his special favourites, and of those thirteen Lhacho Drolma was most dear to him.

The Master of Truth, Lord of Beings, Kunga Legpa, travelled on through the province of Tsang. He took lodging for a night in a small village called Nyug in the house of one Abo Tseten. This man had been a prince, son of the chieftain of Lhatsuk, but he had lost his fortune and had been struck down by leprosy. His wife, Samdron, who was highly talented, had been sent to her betrothed when she was very young. When she grew up to maidenhood, disgusted with her husband, she wished with all her heart that a strong young prince would come to rescue her.

'Once I was a prince, son of a king whose power had no limit,' the Lama's host told him, 'but my luck ran out, and now I live in constant anxiety about how we shall next eat and drink. My wife and son hate and despise me, and my body is diseased. Am I not the most miserable of men?' and he began to cry.

To comfort both husband and wife the Lama decided to tell a story. 'Come here, Samdron!' he called, 'And bring some chung with you. I have a tale to tell.' She brought his chung and he began the story:

Once upon a time, there was an Indian king called Virtue. He was childless until old age when his wife bore him a son who they named Only Son and Heir. When they took him to a soothsayer they were told that disaster threatened the child's life unless he left home for seven years. When he reached manhood they arranged for his departure, bestowing upon him the Sovereign Gem of Kings before he left to wander the country alone.

One day, crossing a wide plain, he came to a spring where

he drank and lay down to sleep. While he was sleeping, the Gem fell out of his nose and into the spring, where the Naga Serpents took charge of it. Bereft of the protecting Gem, he was struck down by leprosy and reduced to abject poverty. Further disaster overtook him when he was accosted by two men who had seen him wearing the Gem in his nose and believing it to be the stone that they themselves had lost, they threatened to put out his eyes unless he handed it over to them. Unable to do so, and unable to convince them of the truth of his story, they blinded him.

The blind leprous beggar groped his way to a happy valley, where he sat down to beg outside the king's palace.

Now the king of that country had three daughters, and it was the time of the annual singing and dancing display. The king sent his daughters to it decked out in full regalia. Before they left he admonished them to distinguish themselves, as in the past, as the most beautiful and accomplished participants. And so it happened, the youngest daughter particularly distinguishing herself. When they returned, the king asked them if indeed they had been the stars of the show.

'We certainly were!' the girls replied.

'And was it through my grace or your own merit?' demanded their father.

'It was through your grace,' replied the two eldest, but the youngest insisted that it was through her own merit. The king became angry.

'I deck you out in the finest jewellery and give you horses to ride, and you still think it was on your own merit that you succeeded,' he raged. 'If you insist that your merit is so great, I will give you to that blind beggar sitting at the gate.'

'If that is what fate has in store for me,' said the youngest, who was the most beautiful of the daughters, 'so let it be!'

Her father grew still more angry and took her down to the beggar saying to him, 'I am the king of this country and this is my daughter who I betrothed to Only Son and Heir, the son of King Virtue, but she is contrary and insolent, so she shall be your wife.'

The beggar sang in reply:

> 'I am a blind, low caste leper
> Unworthy of the King's daughter.

I mean no disrespect or disobedience,
But please be tolerant, O king!'

The princess answered him:

'One cannot escape one's fate;
All depends upon previous karma,
And nobody knows what Fate has in store.
Don't be distressed. I'll carry you along.'

So she carried the leper away on her back, becoming a beggar herself. One day they were resting by a spring on a wide plain, the same spring in which the prince had lost his Gem. He drank deeply, and laying his head in his wife's lap he slept. While he was sleeping his wife noticed a snake come out of his nose and awoke him, asking him what he was dreaming.

'I dreamt that blood, pus and mucus were draining out of my body,' he told her. After she had recounted what she had seen, he understood that it portended the end of his disease, and he asked her to look for his Gem in the spring. Through the power of their combined virtue she found it, and touching it to his eyes his sight was restored. He found himself a prince again, more handsome than before, and his wife, the princess, sang this song in her joy:

'EMA! How wonderful this is!
Tied to a miserable leprous beggar,
A contemptible man without his full powers,
I have watched the vicissitudes of karma dispassionately,
Free of disdain for him, bestowing him honour,
Befriending him in his disgrace,
And today he is revealed the son of a god.
Where is your homeland? And who are your parents?
Tell me today all you have hidden before.'

The prince sang in reply:

'O virtuous woman of portentous lineage!
The land of my birth is Magadha[17]
And my father is the good King Virtue,
To exhaust the karma of my previous life
I was destined to suffer for seven years.
Now we should go to Magadha,
For as an only son I must rule the kingdom.
Lovely and gracious lady accompany me!'

So they returned to Magadha, where the king and queen threw off their mourning and joyfully welcomed the prince and princess. Taking up the reins of government, the prince established the Ten Virtues[18] as the law, and his subjects became happy and prosperous.

One day the prince suggested to his wife that they should visit her father to offer him the gifts due to him for his former grace and favour. The princess put on her full regalia, and with an army of elephants, chariots, cavalry, and infantry, they marched to her father's kingdom. Her father, seeing an army approaching, was desperately frightened. Some of his men donned armour while others fled. The princess went ahead of her entourage, and approaching her father, who failed to recognize her, she dispelled his fears:

'Listen to me, my father and king!
I am the daughter you abandoned long since.
That leprous beggar who sat at our gate
Was the son of the good King Virtue of Magadha.
He found his precious Gem and his sight was restored,
And his bad karma exhausted, his disease was cured.
Now he rules his people righteously.'

She related her story in detail, and then asked her father to prepare a suitable reception. He entertained them lavishly with music, song, and dance, and their happiness was boundless. 'Is this happy occasion the result of your grace or my merit?' the princess asked her father.

Her father was silent for a moment and then replied:

'At first you were both very rich,
Then you were both very poor,
And now, finally, you have both gained power and wealth.'

The Lama finished his story, and then said to Abo Tseten and Samdron, 'Samdron! learn from this parable not to despise your husband or look for another. If you restrain your resentment, like the princess of my story, you will eventually find happiness. And you, Abo Tseten, need not be so depressed. Like the son of King Virtue you will finally find contentment. Give your mind ever to the Lama and to the Three Jewels, and be as virtuous as you are able!'

4 How Drukpa Kunley travelled through East Tsang for the Sake of All Beings

Body of Ultimate Reality, all-pervasive, unchanging delight,
Endowed with the Four Joys, his Speech as sweet as Brahma's,
And with a mind both broad and deep, revealing the perfect way:
We bow at the feet of Drukpa Kunley, Lord of All Beings.

Now the Master of Truth, Lord of Beings, Kunga Legpa, went to Rawa in East Tsang. He stayed there in the house of the Tsang girl Adzomma, singing to the accompaniment of his lute, drinking chung, playing, and making love.

At that time there was an avaricious chieftain called Governor Morang ruling the local fort. One day he caught sight of the Lama from his castle and asked his attendant officer who he was. The officer told him

'Ah yes!' exclaimed the chieftain. 'He is one of those wretched Ralungpas who didn't pay their meat tax last year. It's said that he's a holy man, but he only roams the country getting into trouble. Send a messenger to bring him here.'

A messenger brought Kunley to the castle. 'You are the madman called Drukpa Kunley, aren't you?' gloated the chieftain. 'You Ralung people! Have you forgotten that each of you used to pay Yamdrok Nangkartse a yak and nine sheep in tax, and that you also had to pay a wool and sheep tax to Tsechen? And have I not relieved you of your tax load? Instead of thanking me for that, you killed and ate my musk deer at the Galden Hermitage, and harmed the people of Galden in many ways. You must pay me a hundred carcasses of meat in tax tomorrow without fail.'

'You will be paid according to the account of your virtue and vice by Yama, Lord of Death, who impartially reflects the karma of every being of the six realms[1] in his clear mirror,' the Lama told him. 'However, if you say you must have meat tomorrow, leave your gates open in the morning.'

After he had left, the people wondered how he would accomplish such a task. 'He will surely steal the animals,' they said.

'It doesn't matter how he does it, so long as I get the meat,' said the chieftain. 'Leave the gates open in the morning.'

When the sun appeared over the eastern mountains the following day, a great clamour and cursing was heard approaching from the direction of the Gyangtse Valley, and the Lama was seen driving one hundred and ten musk deer from Galden before him.

'Here is your meat tax!' the Lama shouted to the chieftain. 'Take it if you want it. I can't give it to you tomorrow, but today you can have as many animals as there are in Tibet. If you don't want them I will send them to paradise. That is the Lord of Death's command.'

'Drukpa Kunley, you madman! You are either the devil incarnate or a Buddha's emanation. To herd musk deer like sheep is nothing short of miraculous. However I am not permitted to take meat tax in live animals. I must have dead carcasses,' the chieftain told him.

'That is no problem,' said the Lama, and began cutting the heads off the deer. After he had killed them he began to skin them, piling the bloody carcasses in a heap.

The chieftain became frightened. 'Apau! Apau!' he cried. 'Mad Drukpa Kunley, we have done a great wrong! In the future you and your descendants of the Drukpa clan need pay no Tsang meat tax. Take that meat and sell it in the market place, and liberate those animals' spirits!'

'Yesterday you told me you needed your meat tax, so I drove these animals here. Now you tell me you don't want them. If that's the case these animals can return to Galden.' He snapped his fingers and shouted, 'Go home!' The carcasses arose, found a skin and a head apiece, although some small animals took large heads and some large animals took small heads, and ran back to Galden. Today you can see this strange species of deer with ill-fitting heads around Galden.

The chieftain, his officers and servants, were overcome by profound devotion, and tears ran down their faces. They knelt before the Lama with palms together in prayer. The chieftain said:

> 'Sole refuge of beings, Kunga Legpa!
> The high floating southern clouds of mid-summer
> Are ignorant of the rising and the setting of the sun;
> The piercing cold wind of mid-winter
> Is indifferent to the flowers cut down by the hail;
> The eternal darkness of our ignorance is so immense
> That we failed to perceive that Kunley was an Adept.
> We beg forgiveness for our ignorance and insensitivity –
> Please shut the gates to the lower realms to us,
> And bathe us in your compassion!'

And the chieftain touched the Naljorpa's feet with his forehead. Later, he shaved his head, changed his name, and became a Bodhisattva householder.

The Lama returned to Adzomma's chung house, to his drinking and cavorting. The girls were full of admiration, 'Yesterday you killed those animals and returned them to life, and that gave us great faith in you,' they told him. 'You must certainly have been a Buddha in your past life. Please tell us about it.'

> 'In the rosary of my many lives
> I have taken the form of every creature;
> I remember it only darkly,
> Yet I feel it was something like this:
> Since now I thrive on chung,
> Once I must have been a bee;
> Since now I am so lustful,
> Once I must have been a cock;
> Since now I am so angry,
> Once I must have been a snake;
> Since now I am so slothful,
> Once I must have been a pig;
> Since now I am so mean,
> Once I must have been a rich man;
> Since now I am so shameless,
> Once I must have been a madman;

Since now I am such a liar,
Once I must have been an actor;
Since now my manners are so rude,
Once I must have been a monkey;
Since now I have such blood lust,
Once I must have been a wolf;
Since now I have so tight an anal sphincter,
Once I must have been a nun;
Since now I am so punctilious,
Once I must have been a barren woman;
Since now I spend my wealth on food,
Once I must have been a Lama;
Since now I am so avaricious,
Once I must have been a steward;
Since now I am so self-esteeming,
Once I must have been an officer;
Since now I enjoy cheating others,
Once I must have been a business man;
Since now I am so loquacious,
Once I must have been a woman;
But I cannot tell you if this is really true.
Consider the matter yourselves. What is your opinion?'

'You pretend to be telling us your past lives,' said the girls, 'but actually you are showing us our faults. We thank you for your teaching.'

The Lama travelled on to the Academy of Palkhor Stupa where he found the metaphysicians engaged in debate. Watching the show, his attention was held by a very beautiful woman sitting on the edge of the Stupa.[2] But at the head of the line of monks was an old monk who said to him, 'Your magical powers and signs of accomplishment are astonishing, but, you know, your refusal to bow to the Stupa, and to the monks, is wrong-headed and contrary to the Buddhas' Law.'

'I am an experienced Naljorpa who long ago completed his prostration and confession,' said the Lama. 'But if you wish I will prostrate now.' And he began to perform his prostrations to the girl and the Stupa with this prayer:

'I bow to this body of beautiful clay,
Not counted amongst the Eight Sugata Stupas;[3]

'I bow to the cheeks of the Gyangtse maiden. . . .'

I bow to this marvellous creation,
Not fashioned by the hand of the god of craftsmen;[4]
I bow to these Thirteen Wheels,[5]
Unsurpassed in the Thirteen Worlds;
I bow to the cheeks of the Gyangtse maiden,
Not regarded in the body of the Saviouress.'[6]

'Alala!' exclaimed the monks. 'How crass! This Drukpa Kunley is truly crazy!'

'Since woman is the way that all good and evil enter the world, she has the nature of Mother Wisdom,' the Lama told them. 'And further, when you took your ordination and vows of discipline at the feet of your spiritual preceptor, offering gold and silver without any concern for the future, you entered the mandala between woman's thighs.[7] So I make no distinction between this woman and the Stupa as my object of refuge.'

The laymen who heard him laughed, but the monks gave him black, resentful looks and turned away. 'We are trying to maintain the peerless rules of moral discipline,' said the Moral Guard, 'and you come here making fun of us.' And he took up a stick to beat him. Drukpa Kunley sang this song:

'Proud Kongpo stallion, matchless in style and elegance,
Black Tibetan horse, lifting high its white socks,
Both racing together on the wide open plains –
Aku's Stableboy bear witness –
See which is first to pass the flag!

'Bengali peacock, matchless in fine feathered display,
Tibetan vulture, bird-lord with the wide wings,
Circling high in the empty sky –
Snow Mountain Heights bear witness –
See which bird has the bird's eye view!

'Blue cuckoo in the tree's upper branches, matchless in song,
Red breasted house cock with deafening cokorico,
Both aroused by the season, stretching their lungs –
Old Man of the World bear witness –
See who tells the time correctly!

'Ferocious mountain snow lioness, matchless in pride and
    paw-power,

Striped Indian tiger in the Sengdeng jungle,[8] savage in anger,
Both in the Sengdeng jungle aroused to pitch of cunning fury –
Gomchens and nuns bear witness –
See who truly rules the jungle!

'Palden Stupa abbots and professors of the robe, matchless
     Panditas,
And I, Drukpa Kunley of Ralung, relaxing in the stream
     of events,
All examining our moral performance –
Incontestable Truth bear witness –
See who finally gains Buddhahood!'

Finishing his song, his listeners were overcome with faith
and devotion, and begged the Lama to protect them in this
life and the next.

At Tsechen Monastery (below Gyangtse), where the
monks were conducting the Rite of Confession, the Lama
offered a handful of tea in a cymbal the size of a yak's eye.
'Free tea all round,' he said, making the customary offering.

'There's not enough tea there for three hundred monks,'
they told him. 'Go away!'

The Lama thought he would enlighten them in a playful
manner and began running around the mountain, striding
over boulders and skirting small stones.

'Look at that madman!' cried the monks. 'See how he
runs!'

'This is like your type of practice!' the Lama responded.

'That's nothing to do with our practice!' shouted the
monks. 'That's just your craziness!'

'I will tell you how my gait is like your way of life.'
Kunley explained. 'The Buddha said in the Vinaya that of
the root and branch vows the four root vows are of primary
significance, while violations of the subsidiary vows may
easily be expiated.[9] You people ignore the root vows and
emphasize expiation of minor violations in confessional
rites and so on. Think it over!' he said, and departed.

At Gangchen Chopel Monastery in Tsang, the Lama told
the monks that his tea was not good enough for their
brethren at Tsechen, and that he had come to offer it to
them.

'It's not good enough for us either,' the monks told him. 'Go away!'

Next he went to Tashi Lhumpo,[10] and told the Moral Guard that he wished to make a tea offering. The Guard consulted his superior, who understood that Kunley was an Adept, and told the Guard to do as he was asked. So with the Moral Guard's permission, Drukpa Kunley threw his tea into a vast tea urn together with a lump of butter the size of an egg, and closed the lid with the instruction to keep it closed until he returned. He then descended to the market place and found a chung house, where he drank chung and played with the girls.

Meanwhile the Moral Guard blew his conch to assemble the monks. The cook apologized to them, 'Today we must drink boiled water. A Drukpa made this poor offering and he hasn't even returned as he promised.' But, opening the lid, he was amazed to find the urn full of excellent tea. At that moment the Lama returned.

'It will not rise higher now,' he said, 'and in the future the urn will never be full.' When the tea was being served to the monks, he addressed them: 'I want to tell you that since I only had a handful of tea leaves and an egg-sized ball of butter, as there are over six thousand of you assembled here, the tea will not be so strong. But please drink and enjoy it.' That the tea was excellent in both taste and strength was taken as an auspicious omen, and it is said that the tea of Tashi Lhumpo has retained that same quality until this day.

Later the Lama offered to serve chung to the monks. The Moral Guard forbade it, but the Lama insisted that it would be an auspicious portent. He walked to the middle of the assembly hall and broke wind like a dragon. 'Take your chung please,' he said to the monks, and the whole room was filled with a pleasant odour. The young novices giggled, while the elders covered their noses and frowned. Since that time the back rows where the novices sit have had a holy smell to them, while the front rows of the elders are never reached by the scent of incense.

Drukpa Kunley then decided to return to his homeland of Ralung. As he was ascending from Palnashol, he encoun-

tered an old man called Sumdar who was eighty years old.
He was carrying a painted scroll, a Kahgyu Lineage
Thanka, that had been well executed but lacked the final
gold touch.

'Where you are going?' the Lama asked him.

'I am going to Ralung to ask Ngawong Chogyal to bless
this scroll that I've painted,' replied the old man.

'Show me your scroll!' said the Lama. The old man gave
it to him, asking him his opinion of the work. 'Not bad at
all,' the Lama told him, 'but I can improve it like this.' And
he took out his penis and urinated over the painting.

The old man was shocked speechless, but finally he
managed to say, 'Apau! What have you done, you madman?' And he began to cry.

The Lama rolled up the wet scroll and calmly returned it
to the old man. 'Now take it for blessing,' he said.

When the old man reached Ralung he was granted
audience by Ngawong Chogyal. 'I painted this Kahgyu
Lineage Thanka to gain merit,' he told the abbot, 'and I have
brought it to you for your blessing. But on the way I met a
madman who urinated on it and ruined it. Here it is. Please
look at it.'

Ngawong Chogyal opened it and saw that where the
urine had splashed it was now shining with gold. 'There's
no need for my blessing,' he told the old man. 'It has already
been blessed in the best possible way.' The old man gained
unsurpassable faith and gave loud thanksgiving.

'My scroll has gained a blessing which makes it identical
to Drukpa Kunley himself!' he cried, and went happily
away. It is said that you can still see this painted scroll at the
Dorden Tago Temple in Thimphu.

Continuing his journey to Ralung, he met a sixteen year old
nun (Ani) called Tsewong Paldzom, who had all the signs of
a Dakini. 'Where are you going, Ani?' he asked her.

'I am going to beg alms in the town,' she replied.

The Lama saw that she would bear him a son. 'Ani, you
must give yourself to me!' he exclaimed.

'I have been a nun since childhood,' she replied. 'I don't
know how to.'

'That doesn't matter,' he told her. 'I will guide you.' He caught her by the hand, layed her on the side of the road, and made love to her three times.

After thirty-eight weeks she gave birth to a son bearing auspicious signs. The abbot Ngawong Chogyal, in whose monastery she lived, wished to determine the paternity of the child. When he heard that his father was Drukpa Kunley he told the nun that the Lama was a mad saint and so no virtue had been lost. However, the other nuns in the nunnery said to themselves, 'All other women enjoy sex and now it is made easy for us nuns too!'

'But the abbot will scold us if we become pregnant,' said a nun of little intelligence.

'We will simply name Drukpa Kunley as the father,' she was told, 'and we will be blameless.'

So one nun imitated the next, and doing as they desired, a year later the nunnery was full of children.

'Who is the father of these children?' Ngawong Chogyal stormed. And in each case the answer was the same. 'A kha! kha!' moaned the abbot. 'This madman is responsible for violating the vows of all my nuns!'

When report of this reached the Lama himself, he went to the nunnery and ordered all the nuns to assemble so that he could determine which of their babies was his own. The mothers and babies gathered together, some saying their babies had his face, others his hands, others his feet, his eyes, his nose, and so on.

'If they are my children I will feed and clothe them and take full responsibility for them,' he said, 'but if they are not, I will feed them to the Glorious Goddess[11] to chew on!' So saying he seized his own superior child by the leg and made intercession to the Glorious Goddess:

> 'Glorious Goddess with the Wisdom Eye!
> I, Drukpa Kunley, ever roaming the land,
> Have made love to a garland of young girls,
> But these nuns are lying and cheating –
> If this is my son, protect him,
> And if he's someone else's bastard, eat him!'

And he whirled his son about his head, and tossed him into

an empty field nearby. As he hit the earth a clap of thunder burst from the sky – that field is still called Zhing Kyong Drukda, Protecting-Thunder Field. When the thunder rolled the nuns fled with their babies.

It was at about this time that Ngawong Chogyal saw in a dream that an enemy was trying to kill him, afflicting him with demons. He asked Drukpa Kunley to perform a rite of exorcism to purify his mind. The Lama made an effigy for ransom to the demons and clothed it in robes and other monastic accoutrements. Then he constructed a string rigged trap in which to entangle the demons, and a sacrificial cake which one man could barely carry. He also arranged a mandala, and performed a three day preparatory ceremony of purification. After these three days many people gathered at his house knowing that he would perform a spectacular rite. The Lama enlisted these people to help him. Some he asked to carry the effigy, others the stringed spirit-trap, others the cake, one carried a black pendant, another sacrificial offerings and substances used in the rite. Some he sent ahead chanting, while others swept the sky with black clothes. He himself was wearing a sorcerer's garb and a black hat. His face was smeared with a black herbal paste, and he carried a Ritual Dagger (Phurba) for slaying demons, and a human skull cup for collecting their blood. Accompanied by the clashing of cymbals and the sound of the thigh bone horn, this striking procession moved off to Ngawong Chogyal's house.

Ngawong Chogyal saw that all was proceeding according to custom and was quite relaxed.

'This effigy for ransom is your scapegoat,' the Lama told him. 'Later it will disappear.' And he seated it upon Ngawong Chogyal's throne with due respect. Ngawong Chogyal smiled. Then the Lama went outside and performed a slow dance in invocation of the demons, much to the crowd's delight. When Ngawong Chogyal heard their exclamation, his heart became tremulous. The Lama finished his dance, and returning inside he raised the sacrificial cake and forcefully smashed it down upon the head of the effigy chanting, 'Strike! Strike! Strike Ngawong

Chogyal's lust! Strike his anger! Strike his ignorance! Strike his illusions!' And Ngawong Chogyal was struck with the fear of the world's end, while the people grinned. He looked outside to see what the Lama would do next and saw him perform the heavy stomping dance of suppression of evil spirits before an upturned pot, intoning, 'Bury Ngawong Chogyal's desires!'

Then, turning around, he saw that the effigy had disappeared. 'Today this madman has performed a credible feat of magic,' thought the abbot.

So having demonstrated the efficacy of his ritual exorcism, the Lama returned to his aimless wandering.

The Lama retraced his steps to Palnashol where he enjoyed the hospitality of the chung parlour, drinking and singing. Now in that neighbourhood lived an old woman who was more than eighty years old, and who owned but one cow. In his omniscience the Lama saw that a flat-browed thief was intending to steal it, so he went to the old woman's house, where he found her praying:

> 'OM MANI PEME HUNG!
> Omniscient Lama, Drukpa Kunley,
> Protect me from affliction and pain
> In this life, the next life, and in the Bardo.'

'What are you muttering, old woman?' he asked.

'I am praying to the Lama,' she replied.

'To which Lama?'

'To Choje Kunga Legpa,' she told him.

'Have you ever met him?'

'No, I've never met him,' she said. 'I have only heard his name.'

'I am Drukpa Kunley!' he revealed.

'Are you telling me the truth?'

'Certainly!'

'If you are the real Drukpa Kunley, let us have sexual intercourse!' she challenged.

But she was too old, and the Lama could not get an erection.

'Perhaps it is better if we have spiritual intercourse

'He did the heavy stomping dance of suppression of evil spirits. . . .'

through a few well chosen words,' she said finally.

'If you want spiritual union, learn to recite this,' he suggested.

> 'OM MANI PEME HUNG
> Old Flat-Brow has come,
> OM MANI PEME HUNG
> He sticks out his tongue,[12],
> OM MANI PEME HUNG
> Now he's staying still and silent,
> OM MANI PEME HUNG
> And now he's stealing away.'

After she had learnt this verse by heart, the Lama departed. That night, when the old woman went out to relieve herself, the flat-browed thief came stealing into her yard. He thought that she had seen him because she was reciting the verse that the Lama had taught her. And he thought that she saw him stick out his tongue, and he thought that she saw him lie quietly and finally slink away.

Also by the grace of the Lama, her cow calved, and like a son, it sustained her to the end of her life. Further, it is said that by the Lama's grace she was reborn a Dakini.

Leaving that place the Lama found a house belonging to a wealthy and virtuous man and went inside. 'If you have chung and girls I would like to stay here,' he said to the housewife.

'We have no women, but plenty of chung,' she replied.

'That will do,' he told her. 'I'll stay the night.'

The father of the family was truly devout, his wife was naturally kind, and their daughter was virtuous. The daughter had been recently widowed by smallpox and all three of them were grieving and fasting. The neighbours had tried to comfort them to no avail, and they had continued their weeping and wailing. When the three of them had gathered together, the Lama performed a ritual to lay the ghost of the departed, and then began to assuage their grief.

'In this world of men no one can escape disease, old age, and death. When I was a child, my own father was killed in a family feud and my mother was taken in by her relatives and suffered terribly at their hands.[13] Don't be sad! Listen to this story!'

A long time ago in India, when the Buddha was alive on earth, a man named Graceful Giver and his wife had a beautiful baby son. After the son grew to manhood and married, in order to test the couple's devotion, the Buddha sent a snake which bit the son to death. Later, when the Buddha visited them in the guise of a monk, he found the father joyfully playing dice.

'People are reproving you because you show no sign of sorrow at your loss,' said the monk.

'Don't you know the Scriptures?' asked the man. 'Listen to me!'

> 'In the trees on the peak of the Triple Mountain
> Birds flock together in the evening
> Only to disperse at the first light of dawn[14] –
> Such is the way of all flesh!'

The monk found the dead man's mother singing in the market place. 'People are abusing you because you show no grief over your son's death,' he told her.

'Haven't you heard the Scriptures?' she asked him. 'Listen to me!'

> 'That wandering spirit of consciousness
> Driven by the wind of karma
> I called not hither in the first place
> And sent not hence at the end –
> Such is the way of all flesh!'

Finally, he found the widow singing at her work. 'Aren't you ashamed to be singing happily when your husband has so recently died?' he asked her.

'Don't you know the Scriptures, O monk?' she replied. 'Listen to this verse!'

> 'The wood from the peak of the Triple Mountain,
> The hide from the confluence of the Three Valleys,
> Fashioned and assembled by the boat builder,
> Must one day rot and fall apart –
> Such is the way of all flesh!'

The monk was impressed but sought to test them further.

'They certainly do not grieve at bereavement, but perhaps they will rejoice at a miraculous return,' he thought, and he returned to them, momentarily, their lost son decked in ornaments. But they remained unaffected. Certain then that their realization of Nirvana was profound, he instructed them in meditation, and the three of them gained Buddhahood.

Concluding his story, Kunley continued, 'You three have come together by virtue of your past prayers, and like customers at a stall in the market place, you are destined to part. There is no need for sorrow.'

All three of them realized at that moment that pain was like a dream or hallucination, and bequeathing their property to the monks of a nearby monastery, carrying only religious necessities, they separated. The father went to the White Skull Mountain (Gangri Thokar in Tingri), his wife went to the Chimphu Hermitage at Samye and the widow went to the hermitage at Chushul. Finally, all three of them arrived at the end of the path to Buddhahood.

5 How Drukpa Kunley, the Master of Truth, went to Dakpo and Tsari and arrived in Bhutan

We bow at the feet of Choje Drukpa Kunga Legpa,
Who spoke with the resonance of the illustrious dragon
From the centre of the wafting cloud of Naljorpas
Above the snow mountain chain of the White Lineage.[1]

The Master of Truth, Lord of Beings, Drukpa Kunga Legpa, journeying towards Tsari, discovered a small shack by the pathside near Shar Daklha Gampo. Within he found a dumb idiot called Horgyal and his wife Gayakmo who had all the signs of a Dakini. They were eating tsampa with tea. Seeing that Gayakmo was of excellent spiritual descent, he wished to take her as his consort and set her on the Great Way, so he sang her this song:

'Pale blue monkey swinging in the dry peach tree,
Don't hanker after peaches neither sweet nor sour,
Come and enjoy the goodies in uncle's pocket!'

The girl understood his meaning well enough, and sent off her idiot husband to gather firewood. The Lama sang her another song:

'It would seem by the size of your buttocks,
That your nature is exceedingly lustful.
It would seem from your thin, pert mouth,
That your muscle is tight and strong.
It would seem from your legs and muscular thighs,
That your pelvic-thrust is particularly efficient.
Let's see how you perform!'

'I don't know how to do it,' Gayakmo replied, 'but my vagina is certainly tight because it has never been exercised.'
'Then how does that idiot do it?' asked Kunley.

'He doesn't know the difference between inside and outside,' she told him.

'I know the difference between inside and outside,' said Kunley, and immediately got down to it. Her potential as a Dakini was awoken thereby, and feeling pulled by the religious life, she begged the Lama to take her with him. Seeing that she was a fit vessel for the Teaching, he agreed. When her idiot husband Horgyal returned, she deceived him by saying that she was going up into the mountains to fetch meat and that she would be back by nightfall. So she gathered together a few necessities and faithfully followed the Lama.

Three days later the Lama told her that her husband was still calling out for her, and that the guilt accruing from leaving him haplessly would be a serious obstacle to her spiritual progress. However, he instructed her in meditation for seven days, and then sent her to Tsari Dzachil[2] to begin her meditation practice, telling her that he would follow her shortly.

When he arrived in Daklha Gampo,[3] he found Gomchens, monks and nuns, and laymen and women, devoutly performing prostrations during a period of fasting and religious observance.[4] The Lama went to one side and began his own prostrations with this litany:

'I bow to the unborn, undying Buddha Body of Purity and
   Simplicity;
I bow to the invisible Buddha Body of Consummate
   Enjoyment;
I bow to the ubiquitous Buddha Body of Apparitional Form;
I bow to the Lamas who possess the marks of Buddha;
I bow to the Deity who grants power and realization;
I bow to the Circle of Dakinis who fulfil their duties;
I bow to the Reality Protectors who clear my path;
I bow to the Holy Scriptures which are vast and deep;
I bow to the Saints who are morally disciplined;
I bow to the Philosopher's perspective which has no focal
   point or limitation;
I bow to the Gomchens who are without psychic crutches;
I bow to the Ritualists who are without hypocrisy;
I bow to the Aspirant's Goal which is gained from the start;

I bow to the Votaries who need no vindication.
Thus bowing in humility Enlightenment is gained.

'Now to pay homage to gain power and success:
I bow to the bliss accruing through merit and insight;
I bow to the suffering accruing through evil doing;
I bow to the Naljorpa contented with whatever occurs;
I bow to the ear of the leader refusing to hear petitions;
I bow to the minds of servants refusing to heed instructions;
I bow to the mouths of the rich depriving themselves of the
     food in their larder;
I bow to the pittance of beggars unable to save;
I bow to fornicators discontented with their wives;
I bow to crooked speech and lying talk;
I bow to the ear that heeds youth, ignoring the wisdom of age;
I bow to the cunt of the crone inattentive to death;
I bow to ungrateful children;
I bow to wearers of the cloth who break their vows;
I bow to professors attached to their words;
I bow to gluttonous Gomchens;
I bow to philanthropists with self-seeking motives;
I bow to traders who exchange wisdom for wealth;
I bow to renunciates who gather wealth secretly;
I bow to prattlers who never listen;
I bow to tramps who reject a home;
I bow to the bums of insatiate whores.'

When he finished, some people laughed, some swore he
was crazy, while others said that he merely liked to hear the
sound of his own voice.

'He is neither a madman nor a prattler,' said Gampo
Tridzin Chenga Rimpoche.[5] 'You have all missed the point.
He is a Naljorpa with magical powers and you should all
beg his forgiveness.' They bowed to the Lama and begged
for his bliss-waves. Then the Chenga Rimpoche offered
him liberal hospitality, prepared the guest chamber for him,
and provided whatever he desired for his comfort and
well-being.

'Today I am well-contented and it is fitting that I com-
pose a Song of Intercession from Afar to my Lama,' said
Kunley, and he sang this prayer:

'My Lama Lhaje Sonam Rinchen,[6] look upon me with
     compassion!

Having gained this Precious Human Body through
my past merit, Lama, always remember me!
Transforming all activity on the path into Nirvana,
free from anxiety, Lama, cherish me!
Possessing all I need, free of work and wages, Lama,
safeguard me!
Living in comfortable lodgings, though free of labour
in the fields, Lama, remain with me!
Always regarding my lodging as my home, free of
attachment to it, Lama, protect me!
Identifying the Lama as my own mind, free from
dependence upon others, Lama, remain clear to me!
Letting reality hang loosely, free from mundane pursuits,
Lama, be aware of me!
Unswayed by any argument, free from every persuasion,
Lama, stay with me!
Beyond simulated objects of meditation, free from
distraction, Lama, remain present!
Behaving naturally and spontaneously, free from hypocrisy
and self-deceit, Lama, guide me!
Having achieved the goal at the start, free of all hope
and fear, Lama, guard me!
Comprehending the meaning of SAMAYA, free of the
pitfalls of rigid discipline, Lama, hold me in your eye!
Having the seeds of my desires' fulfilment planted,
free from decision making, Lama, bless me!
Teaching young girls who always listen, free from
contention with their mothers, Lama, live within me!
Parting from my girl friends before they fade, free
from regret and mourning, Lama, gaze upon me!
Always my own steward and treasurer, free from
dependence upon servants, Lama, be with me!
Preferring to remain lowly, free of the pride of Lamas
dominated by the Eight Mundane Preoccupations,[7] Lama, save
me!
Happy to do whatever arises, happy to leave whatever
passes by, Lama, look upon me with compassion!'

At the end of his beautiful song the monks and nuns
served him tea and chung while others fell down swooning
with devotion. Chenga Rimpoche, too, was very pleased:

'Naljorpa contemplating illusion,
Wherever you stay is your Academy,
Wherever you stay is your hermitage.

In your travels throughout the country,
Who have you found the most pious?'

    The Lama replied thus:

I, an ever roaming Naljorpa, visited a Kahgyu Academy,
And in that Kahgyu Academy every monk was holding a jug
    full of chung –
So fearful of becoming a drunken reveller, I kept to myself.
I, an ever roaming Naljorpa, visited a Sakya Academy,
And in that Sakya Academy the monks were splitting subtle
    doctrinal hairs –
So fearful of forsaking the true path of Dharma, I kept to myself.
I, an ever roaming Naljorpa, visited the Academy of Galden,[8]
And in the Galden Academy each monk was seeking a boyfriend –
So fearful of losing my semen, I kept to myself.
I, an ever roaming Naljorpa, visited a School of Gomchens,
And in those hermitages every Gomchen wanted a lover –
So fearful of becoming a father and householder, I kept to myself.
I, an ever roaming Naljorpa, visited a Nyingma Academy,
And in that Nyingma Academy each monk was aspiring to
    perform in the Mask Dance –
So fearful of becoming a professional dancer, I kept to myself.
I, an ever roaming Naljorpa, visited Mountain Hermitages,
And in those hermitages the monks were gathering worldly
    possessions –
So fearing to break my vow to my Lama, I kept to myself.
I, an ever roaming Naljorpa, visited a Charnal Ground and
    outlying areas,
And in those deserted places the Shaman Diabolists[9] were
    brooding on fame –
So fearful of enslaving myself to gods or demons, I kept to
    myself.
I, an ever roaming Naljorpa, visited a Pilgrim Caravan,
And found the Pilgrims engaged in trading –
So fearful of becoming a profit-hungry trader, I kept to myself.
I, an ever roaming Naljorpa, visited a Retreat Centre,
And here the meditators basked in the sun –
So fearing to relax in a small hut's security, I kept to myself.
I, an ever roaming Naljorpa, sat at the feet of an Incarnate Lama
Whose constant preoccupation was his religious treasures –
So fearing to become a collector or miser, I kept to myself.
I, an ever roaming Naljorpa, stayed with the Lama's attendants
Who had established the Lama as their tax collector –

So fearing to become a servant of the Disciples, I kept to myself.
I, an ever roaming Naljorpa, visited the house of a rich man,
Where the slaves of wealth were complaining like Denizens
    of Hell –
So fearful of rebirth as Lord of the Hungry Ghosts,[10] I kept
    to myself.
I, an ever roaming Naljorpa, visited the house of poor,
    lowly people
Who had placed their patrimony and possessions in pawn –
So fearful of becoming a disgrace to my race, I kept to myself.
I, an ever roaming Naljorpa, visited the Religious Centre
    of Lhasa,
Where the hostesses were hoping for their guests' gifts
    and favours –
So fearing to become a flatterer, I kept to myself.
I, an ever roaming Naljorpa, wandering throughout the land,
Found self-seeking sufferers wherever I looked –
So fearful of thinking only of myself, I kept to myself.'

'What you say is very true,' assented Chenga Rimpoche.
The company broke up, each returning to his duty, the
Lama to continue on his way to Jayul.

In Jayul the Lama stayed in the house of the Governor, and
enjoyed lavish hospitality in the company of several Scholars, Gomchens, and monks. They drank chung and con-
versed together.

'You don't wear Lamas', monks' or Sages' apparel,' an
elderly Scholar reproved him. 'You do whatsoever you
please and set a bad example to the common people. You
should find yourself a permanent home and settle down,
instead of wandering around footloose and useless like a
dog. You give all religious people a bad name. Why do you
do it?'

'If I became a Lama I would be the slave of my attendant
disciples, and I would lose my freedom of action. If I
became an ordained monk I would be obliged to keep the
discipline, and who can keep their vows unbroken constantly? If I became a Sage I should engage myself in
discovering the Nature of Mind – as if that was not already
self-evident! Whether or not I am a bad example to anyone
depends totally upon the intelligence of the individual in

question. Furthermore, if a man is destined to spend his time in hell, imitating a Buddha will not save him. And if a man is destined for Buddhahood, the kind of clothes he wears is irrelevant, and his activity, whatever that may be, is naturally and spontaneously pure. Wishing for a permanent home, or becoming fixated upon any single materialistic aim, deflects one from the Path because it strengthens the idea of "I" and "mine". In so far as monks are venerated, their potential for emotional attachment is to that extent greater than the layman's. Although it is usually true that in the first place the motivation for founding a monastery, the desire to establish a place where aspirants can meditate, is laudable, when the need for communal protection gives rise to contention within and friction without, what was originally a sacred fellowship becomes a den of thieves because everyone is overtaken by selfish motivation.'

The Scholars, impressed by this diatribe, approved of his words and thanked him. Then they inquired concerning his vows and the goal to which he was committed. He sang this song in reply:

'Although I cannot constantly pray with sincerity
To the Three Jewels, in which people put their trust,
I vow to maintain the Threefold Commitment[11] –
Keep this vow in your hearts, my friends!
Although I am unable to practise recitation and visualization
To the Deity who grants realization and power,
I vow to desist from cursing and malediction –
Keep this vow in your hearts my friends!
Although I cannot rejoice in sacramental and symbolic offerings[12]
To the Reality Protectors who keep enemies at bay,
I vow not to invite disaster upon my adversaries –
Keep this vow in your hearts, my friends!
Although I cannot meditate without fancy or bias
With a perspective that is always originally pure,
I vow to de-substantialize concrete Name and Form –
Keep this vow in your hearts, my friends!
Although I am unable to order my behaviour
In harmony with the regimen of the quarters of the day,
I vow to avoid an hypocritical front and self deception –
Keep this vow in your hearts, my friends!
Although what I am is not thoroughly comprehended

As the consummate goal – inexpediency abandoned, reality
   realized,
I vow to abandon hope of future attainment –
Keep this vow in your hearts, my friends!
Although I cannot seal an inactive mind
In an experience that is inexpressible and inconceivable,
I vow never to put faith in my mind's conceptions –
Keep this vow in your hearts, my friends!

His audience was profoundly appreciative, and folded
their palms in veneration of the Lama. Then, according to
the varying needs and capacities of the individuals gathered
there, he enlarged upon his teaching, and gave explanation
and elucidation wherever it was required.

The Master of Truth, Lord of Beings, Kunga Legpa, continuing his journey to Tsari, encountered on the way the
Divine Madman of Tsang, called Sangye Tsenchen, and the
Divine Madman of U, called Kunga Zangpo.[13] Finding
their minds in harmony they travelled together to the
Power Place at Tsari. Here they decided to leave behind
some auspicious signs for the sake of future generations.
The Divine Madman of U stamped a clear impression of his
foot in a rock, and the Divine Madman of Tsang impressed
his handprint into a stone as if it was mud.
   'Even my dog has that kind of power,' Kunley mocked,
and he took hold of his dog's leg and imprinted his paw
mark into the rock. These three prints can be seen there even
today.
   These three Herukas[14] showed great respect for each
other's powers as they displayed various miracles and mar-
vels. Finally, before parting ways, they performed circumambulation of the shrine at its base, shoulder, and apex, in
an instant.

The Lama asked the local people if they knew the whereabouts of the Dakpo girl Bumo Gayakmo. He was told that
an avalanche had blocked the path to the cave where she had
gone for meditation, and that she was presumed dead as she
had had only three days supply of tsampa with her when she
left a year before. The Lama then performed a Sacramental

Rite of Offering to the Gods and Protectors, and finding the path open, he set out in search for her. He found her meditating serenely with eyes unblinking.

'O Gayakmo!' he called. 'How are you?'

She replied immediately:

> 'I take refuge in the Gracious Lama,
> In you, the Lama whose teaching is so profound!
> I, the nun, sit in constant meditation
> To gain Buddhahood in this lifetime.
> Is it really possible?'

The Lama stayed with her for three days giving her advice. Not long after he left, Gayakmo attained a Body of Clear Light.

Drukpa Kunley continued on to Jayul where he found a company of intoxicated, Small Tent People[15] from Bhutan, singing songs and drinking chung on the roof of the Jayul Fort during a Sacramental Offering to the Gods and Protectors. The Governor Chogyal Lingpa was also present and enjoying himself. Kunley joined them and was offered chung. Later, he was asked to sing them a happy song, and he sang them this:

> 'Happily I am no common ritualist Lama
> Gathering followers, power and wealth,
> Without time to experience the fullness of life.
> Happily I am no scholarly monk
> Lusting for novice lovers,
> Without time to study the Sutras and Tantras.
> Happily I do not stay in a Mountain Hermitage
> Entranced by the smiles of the nuns,
> Without time to ponder the Three Vows.
> Happily I am no Black Magician
> Taking the lives of other people,
> Without time to cultivate Compassionate Mind.
> Happily I am no Shaman of the charnal ground
> Lending myself to gods and demons,
> Without time to sever the root of confusion.
> Happily I am no householder or father
> Fighting to put food in dependants' mouths,
> Without time to wander in pleasant places.'

He was served more chung, and that night he stayed with the nun Yeshe Tsomo. After a few days he went on to Lhodrak.

Travelling through the district of Lhodrak, he met the Adept Takrepa.[16] 'I would dearly like to sing you a song of praise,' the Adept told him, 'but I don't know how to begin. Please sing one yourself for me.'

'I have no virtues to extol,' the Lama replied, 'but I'll sing you a song anyway.'

> 'Dancer in the indestructible stream of magical illusion,
> Unifier of the welter of inconsistencies and absurdities,
> Power-holder turning the Wheel of Bliss and Emptiness,
> Hero perceiving all things as deception,
> Nauseous Recalcitrant disgusted with temporal attachment,
> Little Yogin piercing others' illusory projections,
> Vagabond selling Samsara short,
> Light-traveller making his lodging his home,
> Fortunate Wayfarer perceiving his Mind as the Lama,
> Champion understanding all appearance as the mind,
> Diviner of Relativity knowing unity as multiplicity,
> Naljorpa tasting the one flavour of all things –
> These are some of the masks I wear!'

Then Drukpa Kunley visited the Power Spots of Drowolung (where Marpa lived and where the Kahgyu Tradition originated), Saykhang Chutokma (the ten story tower which Milarepa built), the cave of Tanyalungpa, and other places, before climbing over from Karchu to Bumthang[17] in Bhutan,[18] where the Second Buddha, Orgyen Padma Sambhava, left his imprint in a rock upon which he had sat in meditation. Here he made demanding eyes at the Bhutanese girls.

'A Tibetan Naljorpa has arrived,' they told each other. 'Let's take him chung and make love with him with body and mind.'

But while the Lama was singing and drinking with the girls, a king of the Mon Chakhar line, King Iron Staff's dynasty, heard of him and tried to poison him, albeit unsuccessfully. Then he tried to shoot the Lama with poisoned arrows, but he missed his mark. After this second failure the king recognized him as an Adept, and paid him profound reverence. Interpreting this event favourably the Lama had a small temple built there which was called Monsib Lhakang. He appointed a Lama to spread the Teaching, and ordained thirty monks. This was the beginning of the spread of the Drukpa Kahgyu Tradition in the eastern borderlands.

He deflowered the virgins[19] of Bhutan, and ever since then consorts with such soft skin, and with such strength to carry loads, cannot be found elsewhere. He taught both men and women the doctrine of karma according to their varying capacities of comprehension and their levels of devotion, and gave them instruction upon recitation of the MANI and the GURU SIDDHI mantras.

In explanation of his behaviour he told them, 'I didn't come here to seduce the girls of Bhutan because I was sexually frustrated. Rather, although I have little power, I came to show you the little that I have; and although I have little benevolence, I came here to offer you some token of virtue. And I didn't wander here seeking food and clothing, for as you have seen, I have refused everything offered to me. Even if you were to offer me a load of capsicum,[20] I would refuse it.' The people were well-content with his words.

Going in search of the Enlightened Poet of Bumthang,[21] Kunley found him discoursing upon a high throne in the market place. The Lama collected together a group of children, and climbing upon a large rock, he began to mimic the Poet.

'I am here to explain the Vision, the Spontaneous Action and the Meditation of the Great Perfection,' said the Poet when he noticed Kunley. 'What are you doing, beggar?'

The Lama sang this song about the Vision and Meditation of the practitioner of the Great Perfection:[22]

'Although the Tise Mountain towers high into the sky,[23]
It must boast a turquoise-maned snow lion;
Although the Vision of the Great Perfection is exalted,
The aspirant must discover the nature of mind for himself.
Although the ocean bed is very deep,

Even fish must learn how to swim;
Although the Sutras' conceptions are profound,
The initiate must develop meditative insight himself.
Although Spell-Mothers, sources of treasure, abound,
Most prefer a monkish sweetheart;
Although the teaching upon discipline is subtle,
Many profound Tantras are of ultimate import.'

The Poet sang this in reply:

'The emptiness in the seeing which is called Vision
Transcends definition as something or nothing;
When "seeing", is there nothing there?
But if there *is* an object of sight, there is no Vision.

'The profundity that is called Meditation
Lies beyond both the presence and absence of mental images;
When there is no mental image, there is no object of meditation,
And when there is a point of reference, there is no meditation.

'He whose moral action is called Spontaneous Activity
Has gone beyond the possibility of choice;
When there is bias and discrimination, there is no perfect action,
And when there is no accepting and rejecting, where is moral
    action?'

The Lama answered with this verse:

'Realizing this Vision of sublime sameness
Ultimate compassion is discovered.
This Meditation which is illusion-free non-meditation
Centres you in the mind's original disposition.
This Spontaneous Activity embracing each moment
Does not discriminate between good and bad situations.'

The Poet was delighted and took off his hat. 'You are
truly an exalted fellow,' he said. 'Please tell me the name of
your Lama, what path of practice you have been taught, and
what has been your spiritual discipline.'
The Lama gave him this reply:

'AHO NGA EGO!
I found a great monk who became my Lama,
And I begged him for the Mahayana Teaching upon the
    Bodhisattva Vow;

Through the practice of the meditation of cherishing others
　　and humbling myself,
I gained the good karma of Compassionate Mind.
I found a Diamond Being[24] who became my Lama,
And I begged him for the initiatory experience of the Four
　　Empowerments;
Through the practice of uniting "Creation" and
　　"Fulfilment" meditation,[25]
I gained the good karma of a Deity in Paradise.
I found All-Embracing Sublime Delight who became my Lama,
And I begged him for teaching upon Original Mind;
Through the practice of unforced attention to whatever arose,
I gained the good karma of entering boundless free space.
I found a Library that became my Lama,
And I begged for direction on the way to universal synthesis;
Through the practice of integrating all experience
I gained the good karma of perceiving purity in all forms.'

　'You are a Naljorpa who has realized the nature of
Emptiness,' the Poet told him. 'What is your family, what is
your spiritual lineage, and what is your name?'
　The Lama replied:

'The name of my line and vestiture are one –
The lineage of Tsangpa Gyarus;
The lineage of my spiritual realization
Descends from Mahamudra;
And my name is Crazy Dragon, Kunga Legpa.
No vagabond begging food and clothes,
But rejecting my home and my family
I wander on never ending pilgrimage.'

　The Poet offered him his best hospitality and he stayed
there for some days discoursing upon Dharma.

Drukpa Kunley then left Bumthang and returned to Tibet
through Lhodrak. Coming down into Gadra in Yamdrok,
he was drinking chung and talking to the Gadrawas when
he was challenged to an archery contest by some very
strong and skilful sportsmen.
　'What should be the stakes?' asked the Naljorpa.
　'You put your horse and clothes down against our crop,'
suggested the Gadrawas, thinking that it would be an easy

victory over a weak beggar. The Lama agreed to their suggestion. The Gadrawas loosed their arrows, missed the target, and lost the match. Then they brought meat and chung, telling him to take it as the fruit of victory.

'We'll stick to the original wager,' the Lama responded. 'You cannot alter the stakes after the match.'

'Then the fish in the river are yours,' he was told. 'That is our harvest.'

'Yah! Yah!' said the Lama complacently, and straight-away began to write this letter:

'OM! On the order of the Lord of Death,
AH! By leave of Unborn Space,
HUNG! By the power of Truth Itself,
From Drukpa Kunga Legpa to Tsomen Gyalmo, the Serpent Queen.
Through victory in an archery contest with the Gadrawas, I have won the fish in the river. Henceforth, do not permit any fish, from those as large as a boat to those as small as a needle, to surface. I hold you to this order until I write to countermand it. Dispatched from the Immense Palace of Clear Light on the seventh day of the fifth month of the year of the dog.'

He threw this missive into the river, and soon after not a fish was to be seen.

After a month had passed, the starving people came to him bearing gifts. 'You are a Bodhisattva with the good of all beings at heart, Precious Master of Truth,' they said. 'Please do not starve us to death like this.'

'I am caught between two millstones,' replied the Lama. 'I will write to Yama, Lord of Death, to clarify this issue.' And he wrote this letter:

I kneel humbly at the feet of the Judge of Karma, Master of Truth, Lord of Death, appointed by the Omnipresent Buddha to weigh good against evil actions. It gives me great joy to hear that your methods of judging virtue and vice are so exact. I would appreciate your judgment upon the following problem: one month ago I won the fish in the river from the Gadrawas in an archery contest, and now they come to me starving, asking me to release their fish. Is it better to save the lives of the fish or to feed the Gadrawas? Please send me a detailed judgment at your convenience.

'. . . thinking that it would be an easy victory over a weak beggar. . . .'

Dispatched by Drukpa Kunley in the human world at Drampagang.

The letter was sent and a reply came immediately:

I have received a letter from Drukpa Kunley, and I have perused its contents. This is my judgment: All beings must suffer the consequences of their actions. These fish are reaping the harvest of their past karma, and there is little that we can do to save them. It is unfortunate that they were not born in the Lake of Yamdroktso, but until their karma is exhausted they must retain their fishly bodies here. Further, if the Gadrawas do not eat fish they will kill other animals and birds for food. It is better if they eat fish, but they should not throw the live fish on to the sand to die without first cutting the nerve behind the gills. Sent from the Court of Yama in the City of the Iron Skull.

As soon as the Lama received this letter, he wrote to the Serpent Queen, Tsomen Gyalmo:

With reference to my previous letter concerning the freedom of the fish in the river, I have sought Yama's judgement in this matter and received in reply an order to release the fish. Therefore, I hereby rescind my previous command and oblige you to give the fish their freedom to surface.

Soon after he sent this letter, the fish appeared in the river as before.

6 How Drukpa Kunley bound the Demons of Bhutan and directed the Aged of that Land to the Path of Liberation

We bow with reverence to the Glory of Kunga Legpa,
Naljorpa exterminating every subject/object dichotomy,
Taking the life of every last delusion spontaneously,
Piercing the heart of the dualizing factor with the arrow of
     non-duality.

When the Master of Truth, Lord of Beings, Drukpa Kunga Legpa, was staying at Lady Semzangmo's house in Nang-katse in the province of Yamdrok, he had a dream. He dreamt that a woman dressed in a yellow skirt, and holding a flaming sword, said to him, 'Drukpa Kunley, it is time that you fulfilled the prophecy that foretold the conversion of the people of Bhutan, and the magical purification of that land. In Bhutan you will establish a family which will serve the Drukpa Tradition to great advantage in the future. You must shoot an arrow to the south early in the morning as a harbinger of your coming.' So saying, she disappeared, and Kunley awoke.

The Lama recognized this as a divine revelation of the Smoky Goddess.[1] Early the next morning he strung his bow and loosed a wailing arrow into the southern sky. 'Fly southwards to benefit all beings and the Tradition,' he intoned, 'and land at the house of a blessed, heaven-favoured girl.'

The land of Yamdrok thrilled to the sound of Drukpa Kunley's arrow. 'Why is the dragon roaring in winter?' cried the people.[2]

'It's the sound of Drukpa Kunley's arrow,' shouted the children.

The arrow landed upon the roof of the house belonging

to the wealthy and devout highlander, Topa Tsewong, in Dramwokma in the district of Topa Silung[3] in Bhutan. The family ran outside fancying an earthquake until they found the arrow still quivering on the rooftop, and realized what had made the house shake. Tsewong's young wife was filled with foreboding.

'There is no need for black thoughts,' said Tsewong. 'This omen portends a son for us. Wash your hands and bring the arrow inside.'

The girl wrapped it in silk, and taking it into the shrine room, placed it upon the altar.

Meanwhile, Drukpa Kunley was coming down from Nangkatse to look for his arrow. He crossed the Phari Tremo La Pass,[4] and descended into the Southern Valleys, a true haven for mankind. At Wodo Rock (between Phari and Paro) he found some travellers camped by the rock, and asked them if he could join them for the night. They indicated the door of a cave. Before they slept that night, he heard them mutter, 'Have mercy upon us Lord Demon of Wodo!'

Before the Lama slept he said, 'May I myself be merciful!'

In the middle of the night he was awakened by a fierce demon with his hair flying behind him in the wind. 'Who are you to talk about mercy?' demanded the demon. 'What do you have that is so special?'

'I have this!' replied the Lama, showing the demon his steel hard penis.

'Ah! It has a head like an egg, a trunk like fish, and a root like a pig's snout,' exclaimed the demon. 'What strange beast is this?'

'I'll show you what kind of beast it is!' Kunley told him, and swung his Flaming Thunderbolt of Wisdom at him, hitting him in the mouth and smashing his teeth back into his head. The demon fled, but returned later in a peaceful frame of mind. The Lama explained the Teaching to him and after imposing deterrent promises upon him, the demon was bound to service of the Buddhas. Thereafter, the Demon of Wodo no longer harmed travellers.[5]

Below Shingkharab (towards Paro) the Lama went to a place which he knew was inhabited by a demoness addicted to human flesh. He waited under a tree, and finally the demoness approached him in the form of a beautiful woman.

'Where have you come from?' she enquired.

'From Tibet,' the Lama told her. 'And you? Where is your home and what are you doing here?'

'I live on the pass,' she explained, 'and I come down into the valley to find food and clothing.'

'What do you eat and what do you wear?' the Lama asked her.

'I eat human flesh and wear human skin!' she replied menacingly.

'Then put this on!' said the Lama, unrolling his foreskin and covering the girl with it. 'In future may you be drenched with rain in the summer and frozen by ice in the winter!'

The demoness was rendered completely helpless, bound by the Lama's blessing.

Descending from Chuyul in eastern Paro district the Lama found his reputation preceding him like the glow of dawn heralding the rising sun. He discovered an old woman, at least one hundred years old, circumambulating a Stupa, muttering the MANI mantra to herself and praying for the Lama's blessing.

'What Lama are you praying to?' Kunley asked her.

'To Drukpa Kunley,' she told him.

'Could you recognize him if you saw him?' he said.

'I've never seen him but I've heard talk of him, and I have great devotion for him,' replied the old woman.

'What would you do if you found him standing before you now?' insisted the Lama.

'I am an old woman and my body is a decrepit thing, but I have chung and food in the house which I would offer him,' she said. 'But it is very unlikely that I could be so fortunate as to meet him.'

The Lama revealed his identity to her, and in her ecstasy she wept and touched his feet with her forehead. 'I take refuge in you in this life and the next!' she repeated over and over. Then she took him to her house and offered him the seven measures of chung that she had ready, and while he was drinking she asked him if she could call her neighbours, elderly widows like herself, to pay their respects. The Lama assented and a little later several old women arrived, each carrying a jug of chung to offer him.

After some time, when he had become thoroughly intoxicated, he called the old lady of the house. 'How much devotion do you really have in me?' he asked her.

'There is no limit to my faith in you,' she replied. 'If you want my life, take it!'

'Would you really give me your life?' asked the Lama.

'I would do anything for you!' insisted the woman.

Now Drukpa Kunley knew that the old woman's time had come, and that the Lord of Death had sent his messengers to fetch her that very night. 'If you are ready for death, raise your arms and show me your ribs,' he directed.

She did as he told her, and picking up his bow and arrow he shot her through. 'Murder! Murder!' screamed the other old women. 'Fly! Fly!' And they scattered up and down the valley sides.

Later a crowd gathered, stunned and astonished. Someone began to swear at him. 'You miserable Tibetan savage! You murderer! Why did you kill this harmless old lady!' Others wept and wailed.

'He is my Lama, and I have complete trust in him,' whispered the dying woman from the floor. 'He is my best friend. Do not treat him like an enemy.' And so saying, she expired.

The Lama carried her corpse into a storeroom, and leaving it there upon a bench, he sealed the door, instructing the people to make sure that it was kept locked for seven days, whereupon he would return.

After six days, however, the old woman's son returned to his home and was told how his mother had mistaken a Tibetan beggar for the Lama Drukpa Kunley, and how the beggar had killed her in a drunken fit, and then locked her corpse in the storeroom.

'Ah! these wretched Tibetans!' the son raged. 'They come

here demanding our hospitality, murder their benefactors, and calmly lock up their victims' corpses to rot.' And he broke open the door of the storeroom. To his surprise he found a pleasant odour permeating the place and the corpse transformed into rainbow light, except for the big toe on the right foot.

At that moment the Lama returned and bit the ear of the old woman's son who had disobeyed his instruction and opened the door prematurely. The unfortunate son was struck dumb, but eventually he found his tongue and praised the Lama with thanksgiving and deep devotion.

'Whether you are grateful or not is irrelevant,' the Lama told him. 'Your mother is now living in a Pure Buddha Land, and that is the important thing.'

Travelling down from Paro Valley towards the Indian plains, the Lama passed a house in which the funeral feast of a woman called Akyi was being celebrated. Seeing him pass by, the relatives of the deceased called to him to join them in their drinking.

'It's good to drink chung in the hot season,' he said, and straightaway began throwing it back.

After he had become totally inebriated, they said to him, 'You are a holy man, aren't you? You can carry the corpse up to the cremation ground.'

'You rogues!' he cursed them. 'I'm no beggar looking for dog's work! Don't you know the proverb, "Although I've eaten my fill, I'll not carry the corpse; although I'm happy I'll not beat the clay!"' [6]

'We are sorry,' he was told. 'You are quite right. But the dead woman is very fortunate in your presence, and it would be very kind of you to assist her through the Bardo.' [7]

'Yah! Yah!' said the Lama. 'If that's how it is, I'll do what's necessary. Where is the cremation ground?' They pointed high up on the valley side. 'Bring me a stick!' he ordered. Taking the stick he began to beat the corpse, chanting:

> 'Don't sleep, old woman! Get up! Get up!
> Arise from this mess of misery!
> You came into this world without purpose

And you are leaving it the way that you came!
You drop your body in front of your sons
But still you have no pall-bearer!
Without your precious clothes that once hid your shame
Nauseating fluids dribble out of you!
Don't lie there, old woman! Walk on!
Walk down the Path of Release!'

And the corpse arose, bent and twisted, and started up the path followed by the Lama with his stick. When they reached the cremation ground the corpse folded its hands and thanked the Lama for showing it the way to salvation. Then it lay down and awaited the fire.

'It is true,' the Lama told the dead woman's relatives. 'She has gained release from Samsara. Now burn the corpse!'

The funeral guests begged him to stay and eat with them. They showed him a pig's head, praising it as a great delicacy, asking him if they should cook it for him. He told them to place it before him, and then pointing at it with his ger he chanted:

'Carcass of pork in the cellar –
Headless and tailless, covered in hair –
And this head with a snout like a donkey's penis,
Get up and go together!
Follow the old woman, now!'

And the people watched as the head dissolved in light and disappeared, spiralling into the western sky. Then the Lama departed without eating.

At Gangtakha (near Kyichu Temple, Paro,) the Gangtak Lama, named Tsewong, begged him to consecrate his new house, and to bless it with whatever auspicious augury would bring good fortune. The Lama made this prognosis:

'Since the door is solid like the mountain
The house will be blessed with endurance;
Since bows are hanging on the pillar
The house will be blessed with wealth;
Since the beams on the ceiling are straight
The house will be blessed with righteousness;
Since the house is roofed with slate
It will be blessed with security.'

And he added, 'This house will be blessed with many inhabitants and many corpses.'

'Akha kha!' they moaned. 'Don't say that!'

'Then let there be few inhabitants and few corpses,' the Lama amended.

Due to that final augury the family became extinct, and today the house stands ruined and empty.

The Lama Kunga Legpa decided to go to bind the Demon of Wong Gomsarkha (in the Thimphu district), who was threatening to exterminate the people of that area. From an inaccessible hiding place high up the valley, this venomous Serpent Demon had terrorized the inhabitants living on the terraces by the river, carrying them off at night, until only one old woman remained. Kunley entered the demon's territory and lay down using his bow and arrows and long sword as a pillow; he placed a pot of tsampa beside him, sucked in his stomach, smeared tsampa on his behind, and gave himself an erection. Lying on his back, he relaxed and awaited the demon, who was not long in coming.

'Adzi! Adzi!' exclaimed the demon. 'What is this? I have never seen anything like it! But perhaps it's edible.' He called loudly to his Elemental Slaves, who immediately descended upon the area in inconceivable numbers like flies on rotten meat. Some of them thought the body was dead, and others thought it was still living.

'We had better not eat it if we don't know what it is,' said the Phuya Fiend. 'The body is warm, so it cannot be dead; it isn't breathing, so it is not alive; there's tsampa in that pot, so it can't have died of starvation; its belly is empty, so it couldn't have died of over-eating; there are weapons under its head, so it's unlikely it died of fear; its penis is still erect, so it must have been alive recently; it has worms in its anus, so it couldn't have died today. Whatever it is, it looks unhealthy for us. We should leave it alone.'

'Whatever we do,' said the Serpent Demon, 'we should eat the old woman today. Let's meet at her door at night-fall.' Agreeing upon this plan, they dispersed.

The Lama arose and went straight to the old woman's house. 'How are you, old lady?' he greeted her.

'You are welcome,' she replied, 'but I am desperate.'

'What's the matter?' the Lama consoled her. 'Tell me about it.'

'Once I was wealthy,' she told him, 'but since no Buddha or Adept has ever set foot in this poor outlandish valley, the demons have run amuck and devoured both men and cattle. I myself do not expect to live through this coming night. You are a holy man and need not stay here. Go away while you can or you will be eaten alive. Tomorrow, if I am not here, you can take anything of value from the house to support yourself or to distribute amongst the poor.' Thus she made her will.

'Things aren't as bad as they seem,' the Lama told her. 'I will stay with you here tonight. Do you have any chung?'

'I had a little but the petty gods and demons stole the moisture,' she replied. 'I don't know whether there is any taste remaining in the grain.'

'Bring the grain and I'll see,' he said.

He was drinking when night fell and the demons arrived at the door. When they began pounding upon it the old woman began screaming in paroxysms of fear.

'You stay up here,' the Lama directed. 'I'll take care of this.' Down below, he took his erect penis in his hand and thrust it through the hole in the door which was big enough to take a fist, and as a Flaming Thunderbolt of Wisdom it rammed into the Serpent Demon's gaping red mouth knocking out four teeth above and four teeth below.

'Something hit me in the mouth!' screamed the demon wildly, and fled down the terraces of the river valley until he came to the cave called Lion Victory-Banner, where a nun called Lotus Samadhi was sitting deep in meditation. 'Naljorma! Something weird hit me in the mouth,' he stormed breathlessly.

'Well, what was it, and where did it come from?' she enquired.

'It was at the old woman of Gomsarkha's house. A strange man who was neither a layman nor a monk hit me with a flaming iron hammer,' panted the demon.

'You have been hit by a magical device,' the nun told him. 'That kind of wound never heals. If you doubt me look

' "We had better not eat it," said the fiend.'

at this.' She raised her skirt and opened her legs. 'This wound was caused by the same weapon. There is no way to heal it.'

The demon put his finger to it and raised it to his nose. 'Akha! kha! This wound has gone putrid, and I suppose mine will go the same way,' he moaned. 'What should I do?'

'Listen to me and I will tell you,' the nun told him. 'Go back to the man who hit you. He will still be there. His name is Drukpa Kunley. Offer him your life, and vow never to harm living creatures again. Then perhaps you may be cured.'

The demon took this advice, and returned to the house where the Lama awaited him. He prostrated before the Lama, and said, 'I am yours to command. I offer you my life.'

The Lama placed his Thunderbolt upon the demon's head and ordained him as a layman, binding him with the lesser vows.[8] He gave him the name Ox-Devil, and invested him as a Reality Protector. Even today he is the Master of Gomsakha, and offering[9] is still made to him.

Ascending from the Lhangtso river valley, the Lama saw the terrifying form of the Lhadzong Demoness approaching him dressed in absurd, unconventional clothing. He immediately erected his Flaming Thunderbolt of Wisdom in the sky and she, unable to bear the sight of that magical tower, changer herself into a Venomous Serpent. The Lama stepped upon her head and the creature was petrified. It can still be seen today in the middle of the main road.

Finally Choje Drukpa Kunley arrived at Topa Tsewong's house, where his arrow had fallen, and stopped to piss against the wall.

'What an enormous cock and balls he's got!' shouted some watching children.

The Lama sang them this song:

'In blue cuckoo summertime your cock is long and your balls
    hang low;
In the purple stag wintertime the head of your penis grows long.
Throughout the year it's a long hungry beast,
But that is the difference between summer and winter!'

Then he entered the house and asked Tsewong for his arrow. Tsewong assured him that his arrow was there and invited him to stay. Suddenly Kunley's eyes fell upon the lady of the house, Palzang Butimo (or Rigden Norbu Dzomma as she was sometimes called), and becoming entranced with only so much as a glance at her divine countenance and full-bloom flower-like face, he sang:

> 'The arrow has certainly not gone astray
> Since it has led me to this voluptuous goddess.
> Tsewong, mine host, please leave us
> I must lay this lady this instant.'

And the Lama immediately prepared to take her. Her husband was enraged and unsheathed his long sword, chanting as he prepared to attack:

> 'I offer you lodging and you steal my wife
> Without barely a courteous word of greeting;
> Without even resting you try to seduce her!
> I've never seen nor heard of such behaviour!
> You may act like that in Tibet
> But we southern folk have no such custom!'

So saying, he threw his sword at the Lama, who caught it in his right hand while grasping Palzang Buti by the neck with his left.

Tsewong was awed, 'I didn't realize you were a Buddha,' he said, and touched the Lama's feet with his forehead. You may take my wife as your own and stay here as my Lama in residence for as long as I live.'

Drukpa Kunley promised to stay for some time, and during that period, through the power of prayer, Phajoisay Sangdak Garton entered Palzang Buti's womb and was reborn as Ngawong Tenzin. When he grew up he became a monk at Ralung and gained power sitting at the Lotus Feet of his Tutor Ngagi Wongchuk. He fulfilled the prophecy of the Dakini by performing the Rite of Generation after founding the Tamgo Hermitage, and gave rebirth to Phajo as his son, Tsewong Tenzin. Yabje Tsewong Tenzin begat the Adept Jingyal and Gyalsay Tenzin Rabgyay, but here this family line ended.[10]

This verse became current during Kunley's stay at

Tsewong's house:

> The Highlander Tsewong loves truth
> Duty-Free Kunley loves Tsewong's wife;
> Good luck to truth-lover and wife-lover!

One day the Lama decided to go and tame the demon of the valley head. He climbed high up the valley side and encountered an old man called Apa Sitha Drugyay cutting peat. Now the Lama knew that Apa was interested in buying some cymbals, and decided to pose as a trader.

'Who are you?' the Lama asked.

'I'm a peat cutter,' Apa told him. 'Where are you coming from, Naljorpa?'

'I'm a cymbal merchant from Tibet,' said Kunley.

'Do you have good quality cymbals?' asked Apa. 'What is their name?'

'Yes they're good quality cymbals. They're called "Clangers," '[11] the Lama assured him.

'Perhaps I will buy them,' said Apa. 'Let me see them.'

'There's a proverb concerning the cymbal business,' said Kunley. ' "You can't say prayers without opening your mouth, and you can't beat a drum with an empty hand!" It follows that we can't do business without chung. Do you have any with you?'

'I have seven measures at my house,' Apa told him. 'I'll fetch it if you continue with this peat cutting.'

So taking up the spade, Kunley began to cut the peat. Soon after, the savage looking demon of the valley jumped upon him. The Lama hit him in the mouth with his Flaming Thunderbolt of Wisdom and then chased him into a huge boulder at Topa Silung Nang. 'Until the end of the world, don't come out!' Kunley ordered, and he sealed the rock with the blood of his nose.

Returning to Apa's house on the valley-side he asked for chung, and after drinking for some time Apa asked to see the cymbals.

'Drink now and we'll do business later,' said the Lama.

'I want to see them now,' Apa persisted.

'Here are your cymbals,' said the Lama, blowing out his cheeks. 'I drink [*rol*] chung and become drunk [*dgah-mo*] and aren't these cheeks cymbals [*rol-mo*]?'

Apa became angry, 'If you don't have any cymbals for sale you can pay for your chung, you beggar!'

'You pay for the chung!' the Lama responded.

'I don't pay for my own chung!' Apa shouted.

'You would be dead now if it wasn't for me,' said the Lama calmly. 'I saved your life by taking your place in the field, and I've given you security by imprisoning the demon of the valley in the Silung Rock.'

'O don't tell me stories about putting demons into rocks,' said Apa scornfully. 'Just pay for your chung.'

'Let's go and see if I'm telling the truth,' the Lama offered, and they walked up to Silung.

Reaching the rock, Drukpa Kunley directed Apa to put his ear to it. 'Please let me out into the valley, Drukpa Kunley!' Apa heard.

'I didn't realize you were a Buddha,' said Apa, amazed. 'Please forgive me. You need not pay for the chung.' And he was filled with faith. 'If you can bind all kinds of demons there's a demoness on Dokyong La pass that constantly menaces travellers, and the people would be eternally grateful if you could subdue her. Many travellers have been devoured by her, and no one will cross after night fall.'

The Lama immediately ascended to Dokyong La pass (between Thimphu and Punakha), where he met an eighteen year old boy from Wong with a cow. 'Where are you from?' asked the Lama.

'I'm from Wong Barpaisa, but it's too late to return there safely. Please help me!' begged the boy.

'Why, what's the matter?' Kunley asked.

'After nightfall the demoness will carry us off,' the frightened boy told him.

'Then you go on home, and I will take care of the cow,' offered the Lama.

'I can't reach home before dark,' said the boy.

'Then put your head in my lap and think of home,' the Lama commanded. The boy did as he was told and immediately found himself transported to Wong Barpaisa.

The Lama tied the cow to a tree and climbed into the branches above it to await the demoness. After darkness she appeared, her mouth gaping and salivating. When she saw the cow she called up the hill to the Sing La Pass Demoness and down the hill to the Hing La Pass Demoness, telling them to come and feast. As they were about to eat, they saw the Lama in the tree.

'Come down and play with us,' they called.

'I won't play with you, you filthy creatures,' he retorted.

They became enraged and kicked the tree down. The Lama grasped his singular Thunderbolt of Wisdom in his hand and spat flame at the two lesser demonesses, but they immediately dissolved into the Dokyang Demoness herself. The Lama then caught her by the hair and dragged her to Drulopaisa (on the Wongdu road). Here she stood up and transformed herself into a red dog. The Lama caught the dog by the ear, covered it with a pile of earth to resemble a woman's breast, and built a black stupa on top of it. He predicted that a temple would be constructed over it at some future time.

Then the Master of Beings, Lord of Truth, Kunga Legpa, decided upon a confrontation with the terrible Long Rong Demoness in order to subdue her, to bind her, and to transform her into a Guardian of the Tradition. As he descended to the river (on the road to Punakha) she saw him coming, and putting on her most fearsome form, she floated in a dazzling cloud of spray whipped up by the eddying river and sang this song:

> 'Come here and listen to me, Naljorpa!
> The celebrated white peak of Tise
> And the deserted Chung Tung,[12] fortress of the wind,
> Are but rock and earth blanketed in snow.
> Are they so marvellous?
> The celebrated white snow lion,
> Lord of Beasts with white fur and turquoise mane,
> Roars ineffectually in the valleys.
> Is he so marvellous?
> The celebrated ascetic, Drukpa Kunley,
> A poverty stricken, wandering beggar,
> Talks nonsense and tells dirty stories.
> What is so marvellous about that?
> Don't expect homage or offering from me!

Tell me by whose authority you have come here,
And who you have come to assist.
What is your spiritual lineage and Tradition?
If you are a Buddha, answer me!'

The Lama sang this reply:

'Listen, you Water Serpent Demoness![13]
Do not treat me with such scorn.
I come here today in answer to prayer,
So keep your mind carefully in check
And give me your full attention.
On the celebrated white peak of Tise,
Five hundred saints abide in serenity;
While on the back of the white snow lion
The Dakinis and Great Mothers ride;
And the whole universe pays respect
To this famous Drukpa Kunley.
This indigent beggar, this vagrant,
Has turned from desire in disgust
And speaking whatever enters his mind,
Outward show is invested with virtue.
Never working, letting reality hang loosely,
Whatever arises is the Path of Release.
It was the Vajra Bearer who sent me here
To release all beings from the Round of Frustration;
And my Tradition is Mahamudra –
Like Jetsun Milarepa
I am a sovereign ornament of every situation.
So, Long Rong Demoness, be content as Protectress!
You daughter of gods, serpents, devils, and demons,
Worthy consort, attractive and charming,
Insubstantial apparition, follow me!
Hold to the blissful Path of Release
With your body, speech and mind
And gain Buddhahood in this lifetime.
Now answer me righteously!'

The demoness adopted the form of a beautiful and seductive
woman, and brought chung to the Lama in a huge crystal
urn and sang him this song:

'Hear me, Duty-Free Drukpa Kunley!
Exalted in race, empowered by Truth,

With a Buddha's heart in an ashen body,
Carrying bow and arrow as Expedience and Insight,
Bearing the Shield of Patience and Tolerance,
Leading a dog to destroy all emotion,
Possessing the power of a Universal Emperor,
I beg you to lead me to a blissful release.
Am I not a celestial ornament?
Above my waist my form is entrancing
While below my waist in my Mandala of Bliss
My muscles are strong, and my upthrust is skilful –
I offer you my art in milking!
For you, a Naljorpa who delights in love making,
And I, a serpent with fervent lust,
This meeting today augurs great joy.
Please stay this night with me here
And I'll offer you my body in devotion.
I beg you to grant me your godly favour!'

She took the Lama to her house and made him offerings.
Then she promised to serve the Tradition thereafter, and
vowed never to harm living beings. Finally, to prepare her
as a suitable candidate for instruction on higher spiritual
union, he purified her through divine sexual play.

On his return from the Long Rong valley, the Lama entered
an arid region which he named Lokthang Kyamo (Arid
Land). Here he met an old man called Apa Gaypo Tenzin.
The old man's sons had left home and all but his youngest
daughter had married and gone to their husbands' homes,
leaving him bored and with nothing to do except follow his
devotions. He prostrated at the Lama's feet.

'I am most fortunate to meet you,' he told the Lama. 'My
elder sons have established their own homes, my youngest
son has entered a monastery, and my daughters have married. I am bored with life and need the teaching that will
prepare me for death. Please instruct me.'

'Yah! Yah!' said Kunley pensively. 'I will teach you a
Refuge Prayer[14] which you must recite whenever you think
of me. There is one stricture which accompanies it – never
discuss it with anyone.' And he taught the old man this
Refuge which gives release from Samsara:

'I take refuge in an old man's chastened penis, withered
    at the root, fallen like a dead tree;
I take refuge in an old woman's flaccid vagina, collapsed,
    impenetrable, and sponge-like;
I take refuge in the virile young tiger's Thunderbolt,
    rising proudly, indifferent to death;
I take refuge in the maiden's Lotus, filling her with rolling
    bliss waves, releasing her from shame and inhibition.'

'Remember to recite this Refuge whenever I enter your
mind,' repeated the Lama.

'I thank you with all my heart,' Apa Gaypo said fer-
vently. 'Now please teach me a prayer that will strengthen
my aspiration.' The Lama taught him this:

'The branches of the Great Eastern Tree grow and grow,
But the foliage's spread depends on the tree's roots' extent.
Drukpa Kunley's penis head may stick, stick in a small vagina,
But tightness depends upon the size of the penis.
Apa Gaypo's urge to gain Buddhahood is strong, so strong,
But the scale of his achievement depends upon the strength of
    his devotion.'

'Keep this prayer in your mind!' Kunley directed him.

The old man returned home. 'Did you meet the Lama?'
his daughter asked him. 'Did you receive his instruction?'

'He gave me a Prayer of Refuge which I learned by heart,'
he replied.

'You are neither intelligent nor educated,' said his
daughter. 'Was it short and concise? Please repeat it for us.'

Apa folded his palms in prayer and began, 'I take refuge in
an old man's chastened penis. . . .' and so on, in exactly the
way that the Lama had taught him. His daughter ran away
in embarrassment.

'Are you crazy!' demanded his wife. 'A Buddha Lama's
words are always quite pure. Either you misunderstood the
Lama or you have forgotten what he told you. And even if
you have remembered the words correctly, it is shameful to
imitate the Lama. You must never repeat this in front of the
children!'

'The Lama told me to repeat it whenever I thought of
him,' Apa insisted, 'and that I will do.'

Later, when the family was gathered for their evening meal, Apa folded his hands and again repeated the prayer. 'The old man has gone mad,' they whispered to each other, and taking their bowls with them they left the table, so that when Apa reopened his eyes he was alone. When his wife returned she told him that he must stay in a room apart if he persisted in his madness. Apa insisted that he would continue even at the cost of his life, so the hayloft in the roof of the house was prepared as his room of confinement, and he moved in there and continued to pray day and night.

About a month later on the evening of the full moon, strains of lute and piccolo were heard through the house. Apa's wife, unable to hear her husband's voice in prayer, grew apprehensive, thinking that perhaps he was crying and moaning in nervous depression. 'Go take your father some chung,' she told her daughter.

The girl went up to the loft with the chung and found only a heaped quilt on the bed. She threw off the quilt and found a sphere of rainbow light with the syllable AH in the centre of it, shining white and radiant.[15]

'Apa! Apa! Apa has gone! Come quickly!' she screamed in superstitious dread.

When the family and neighbours had gathered, the sphere of light flew off into the western sky, trailing behind it the voice of the old man. 'Drukpa Kunley has delivered me into the Potala Mountain Paradise of the Bodhisattva of Compassion. You prudish people must stay here! Give the Lokthang Kyamo to the Lama as an offering.'

When the Lama visited that house, he built a stupa over the spot where Apa had died and put the old man's rosary inside as a relic. Later the abbot Ngawong Chogyal built a monastery around the stupa, and today that monastery is called the Khyimed Temple.[16]

7 How Drukpa Kunley instructed his Consorts in the Southern Valleys

We bow at the feet of the Divine Madman, Drukpa Kunga
  Legpa –
Intoxicated by the divine face of the Goddess Joyous Wisdom,
Recounting whatever occurs with flippant delight,
He is the fool who reveals the lie in the World of Vanity.

When the Master of Truth, Lord of Beings, Kunga Legpa, visited Samten Gang (in the district of Wongdu), he was greeted by the devout nun, Anandhara, Mistress Gyaldzom of Khyung Sekha, the maiden Gokyi Palmo of Wache, Mistress Adzom of Gomto, Namkha Dronma of Pachang, Zangmo Chodzom of Wong Barpaisa, Youthful Kunzangmo, and other girls of Mon who had the fortunate karma of becoming the Lama's consorts. Also present were Lama Paljor of Chang Gang Kha with other devout patrons, and Gyaldzom of Drung Drung with other perverse politicians. These devotees assembled a vast congregation of people from all over Bhutan to witness the magical powers of the Lama.

'We have been told that you are able to perform miracles and feats of spiritual power,' they told him, 'but we have never witnessed them ourselves. We beg you to show us true signs and miracles that we may be convinced of your power and realization.'

Then they served him a goat's head and a carcass of beef, which he devoured with relish. When he had finished he took the goat's head and stuck it upon the headless skeleton of the cow. 'You have no flesh on your bones,' he said to the animal. 'Go up on the mountain and graze!' He snapped his fingers and the beast arose and ran up the valley, to the astonishment of all those present.[1] This species of animal

with a goat's head and cow's body can still be seen in that
valley today. It is called Drong Gimtsey.[2]

Then these consorts and patrons of Bhutan made a further request to the Lama. 'Lama Rimpoche, we beseech you
to bless us, the people of the Southern Ravines, with a
discourse upon the Buddhas' Teaching. We ask that you
give your discourse a name in Sanskrit, that it be serious in
content, but with some touches of humour. Please deliver it
in the language of the common people so that everyone can
understand it, but give it a profound inner meaning. Teach
us the simple message of the Buddha, so that merely by
hearing it we are released from the troubles of transmigra-
tory existence.'

The Lama delivered this discourse:[3]

'In Sanskrit – Nga'i mje sha–ra–ra!
In Tibetan – Bu–mo'i stu–la shu–ru–ru!
This is the discourse on mundane pleasure.

'The virgin finds pleasure in her rising desire,
The young tiger finds pleasure in his consummation,
The old man finds pleasure in his fertile memory:
    That is the teaching on the Three Pleasures.
The bed is the workshop of sex,
And should be wide and comfortable;
The knee is the messenger of sex,
And should be sent up in advance;
The arm is the handle of sex,
And it should clasp her tightly;
The vagina is a glutton for sex,
And should be sated again and again:
    That is the teaching upon Necessity.
It is taboo to make love to a married woman,
It is taboo to make love to a girl under ten,
It is taboo to make love to a menstruating woman
Or a woman under a vow of celibacy:
    That is the teaching on the Three Taboos.
Hunger is the mark of an empty stomach,
A large penis is the mark of an idiot,
Passionate lust is the mark of a woman:
    That is the teaching on the Three Marks.
The impotent man has little imagination,
Bastards have little virtue,

The rich have little generosity:
 That is the teaching on the Three Deficiencies.
A Lama's joy is a gift,
A politician's joy is flattery,
A woman's joy is her lover:
 That is the teaching on the Three Joys.
Sinners hate the pious and devout,
The rich hate loose spendthrifts,
Wives hate their husbands' mistresses:
 That is the teaching on the Three Hates.
For blessing worship the Lama,
For power worship the Deity,
For efficiency worship the Reality Protectors:
 This is the teaching on the Three Objects of Worship.
Pay no respect to mean Lamas,
Pay no respect to immoral monks,
Pay no respect to dogs, crows or women:
 That is the teaching on the Three Rejects.
The Discipline's purpose is to calm and pacify,
The Vow to serve others is to free from self-will,
The Tantra's purpose is to teach unity of polarity:
 That is the teaching on the Three Vehicles.[4]
The starving beggar has no happiness,
The irreligious have no divinity,
The wanderer has no bonds or commitment:
 That is the teaching on the Three Lacks.
He who is without honesty has a dry mouth,
He who is without spirituality makes no offering,
He who is without courage does not make a general:
 That is the teaching on the Three Zeros.
The sign of a rich man is a tight fist,
The sign of an old man is a tight mind,
The sign of a nun is a tight vagina:
 That is the teaching on the Three Constrictions.
The fast talker inserts himself into the centre of a crowd,
Monastic wealth inserts itself into the monks' stomachs,
Thick penises insert themselves into young girls:
 That is the teaching on the Three Insertions.
The mind of a Bodhisattva is smooth,
The talk of self-seekers is smoother,
But the thighs of a virgin are smoother than silk:
 That is the teaching on the Three Smooth Things.
Immoral monks have thin skirts,

Widows and spinsters have thin stomachs and clothes,
Fields without manure bear thin crops:
    That is the teaching on the Three Thin Things.
Kunley never tires of girls,
Monks never tire of wealth,
Girls never tire of sex:
    That is the teaching on the Three Indefatigables.
Although mind is clear, one needs a Lama;
Although a lamp burns brightly, it still needs oil;
Although Mind is self-evident, it needs recognition:
    That is the teaching on the Three Needs.'

And then the Lama continued:

'The Lama without a disciple, the student without persistence,
The pundit without an audience, the woman without a lover,
The master without a servant, the rich man without food,
The farmer without crops, the nomad without cattle,
The monk without discipline, the Gomchen without instruction,
The nun obsessed with sex, the man unable to reach erection,
Wealth sought with the bum, and shy girls panting for sex –
How ridiculous they look! What laughter they raise!'

And again he went on:

'Although the clitoris is suitably triangular,
It is ineligible as devil-food for the local god's worship.
Although love-juice can never dry up in the sun,
It is unsuited for tea to quench thirst.
Although a scrotum can hang very low,
It is an unsuitable bag for the hermitage's victuals.
Although a penis has a sound shaft and a large head,
It is not a hammer to strike a nail.
Though endowed with a human body and shapely,
It is not proper to be mistress to the Lord of Death.
Although your mind may be virtuous and pure,
The Buddhas' Teaching is not accomplished by staying at home.
The teaching of the Tantric Mysteries is most profound,
But liberation cannot be gained without profound experience.
Drukpa Kunley may show you the way,
But you must traverse the path by yourself.'

After he had finished this discourse, the people cried and
laughed, and crying and laughing they left that place with
great faith and devotion. Through his own buoyancy and

benevolence his fame spread throughout the land of Bhutan, and all men and women, monks and laymen, recognized his power and revered him. By virtue of this faith and devotion they became ready vessels for the Buddhas' ambrosia.

When the Lama Drukpa Kunley arrived in Shar Kunzangling,[5] the inhabitants confabulated: 'We should try and bring our demon face to face with Drukpa Kunley,' they plotted. 'No one give him lodging so that he has to stay up in the ruins. We'll take him food up there.'

So, unable to find lodging in the village, the Lama went up to the ruins to sleep, and at midnight he was attacked by a demon that had nine goitres piled one above the other growing out of his neck. Kunley thrust his Flaming Thunderbolt of Wisdom up the demon's rear and sent him fleeing up the hill. Even today near the Orgyen Rock, one can smell burnt meat and hear cries of pain. And although there used to be eighty tax payers in Kunzangling, because the people refused Drukpa Kunley hospitality, now there are only four.

Early one morning, gazing across the valley from Kunzangling to Khyung Sekha, the Lama caught sight of Mistress Gyaldzom swinging her hips and dancing under a sandalwood tree, and he sang this song across to her:

> 'Looking out from Shar Kunzangling
> I see the Dakini of Khyung Sekha
> Swinging and swaying like a goddess.
> She must be Mistress Gyaldzom!
> Today when the sun reaches its zenith
> The Duty-Free Kunley will visit you.
> Fill a yak horn full of the essence of chung[6]
> And we'll tell stories and enjoy love together!
> OM MANI PEME HUNG!'

Later in the day he arrived at Mistress Gyaldzom's door and found her about to go to fetch water. She asked him to wait for her inside.

'You don't need to fetch water,' said the Lama. 'We'll make it run from your own spring!' And he layed her down on the doorstep and made love to her. Afterwards she made him tea and served him well until he was ready to take his leave.

'Stay with me for ever!' she begged him.

'I cannot stay here,' he replied. 'But because your secret place is hairless, I'll return to you for nine days some time in the future. I'll return for another nine days because it is dry. And I'll return for another nine days because your body has no odour. But now I must leave.'

Gyaldzom refused to be put off, and quickly filling a pitcher full of liquor, she followed him. On the top of a hill the Lama stopped, and asked the girl what the surrounding area was called. She told him it was Pangyul and that the name of the upland was Lokthang Kyamo.

'Well, this Pang (out-pour) is an omen, as Lokthang Kyamo (arid land) certainly needs it. Pour out the liquor!' And he started drinking. 'You eastern girls are celebrated singers. Sing me a song!'

Gyaldzom sang this song:

'O Drukpa Kunley! Wandering Naljorpa!
Listen to the song of this maiden Gyaldzom
The mountain meadows turn white in winter
But Crazy Kunley is whiter (happier);
The meadows turn from white to green and green to white
But Kunley, Master of Truth, stays ever white.
The sharp-eyed vulture soaring high
Has no power in its wings,
So when the storm of karma blows
Perforce it must follow the wind.
I, Mistress Gyaldzom of Khyung Sekha,
Powerless to determine my fate,
Destined to wait sadly at home,
Eventually found my true consort –
But this transient meeting leaves me sad.'

The Lama sang this song in reply:

'Listen, Mistress Gyaldzom of Khyung Sekha!
Listen to Kunley's song!
Fire heats icy glacial waters
But Gyaldzom's heart heats faster.
The sun heats water in crevices in the rock

But Gyaldzom's heart heats faster.
Exertion heats juices of the secret spring
But Gyaldzom's heart heats faster.
You may bubble and boil
And I will stay white and happy!'

They sang their songs and parted, but even today that place is called Heart-Warming Country (Lokhol Yul).

The Master of Truth, Lord of Beings, Kunga Legpa, travelled on to Gyengling Nyishar (in the Wongdu district) and stayed with the nun Anandhara, drinking chung, playing with the girls, and singing songs. In between times he taught the Buddhas' Truths. One day after Sharmo Kunzangmo had served him her best chung, she sang him this song:

'EMA! Tibetan Naljorpa, Drukpa Kunga Legpa!
Listen to this sad girl's song!
I feel like the misused wood of a cellar doorstep
Held firmly in place by the door-posts,
Abused by trampling dogs and swine.
Don't leave me here! Take me to Ralung in Upper Tsang
And make me part of the temple, so I may gain Buddhahood.

'I feel like the ill-treated iron on the blacksmith's anvil
Caught by pliers and pinchers, unable to move,
Beaten by the hammer at the blacksmith's whim.
Don't leave me here! Take me to Ralung in Upper Tsang
And make me part of the temple door, so I may gain
    Buddhahood.

'I, miserable Sharmo Kunzang, abused and ill-treated,
Have such love for my parents that I am constrained to remain,
But my cruel husband makes my life unbearable.
Don't leave me here Kunley! Take me to Ralung in Upper
    Tsang
And let me gain Buddhahood in this lifetime.'

The Lama sang this song in reply:

'Listen to me, Kunzang of Sharmo!
While crossing the sky, the sun shines on all four continents,
And wandering Kunley needs no travelling companion.

'The most fortunate tree grows tall in inaccessible southern
   jungles,
Where the axe of the callous woodman cannot touch it.
Better to be a spreading tree than a temple door-post,
And the cellar door-step can be made of stone.

'The most fortunate iron finds the anvil of the blacksmith,
But better a staff or a begging bowl for you than a temple door.
You need not suffer on the sweating, scorched blacksmith's anvil,
When wood and stone can replace the blacksmith's iron.

'You, fortunate girl, born in Gyengling Nyishar,
Need not bear the beating of your ox-like husband.
But rather than become my lover, go into meditation,
And let your sister-in-law replace you as your parents' servant.'

Kungzangmo was struck with faith by the Lama's words
and vowed to do as he advised. After she had received
instruction in both sexual and spiritual intercourse, she
went up to Paro Chumphuk and stayed there for three years
in meditation. Finally, by a fortunate conjunction of the
Lama's grace and her own devotion, she gained a Body of
Light.

At Jenang Wache, as the sun was setting and the Lama was
looking for a place to spend the night, he met the maiden
Gokye Palmo at a spring.

'Please give me lodging for the night,' he asked of her.

'O Drukpa Kunley! You won't find anyone to take you
in. And do you know why? Because in the first place you
demand hospitality; secondly you seduce the lady of the
house; and thirdly you talk dirty. I have no accommodation
or chung to offer you,' said the girl.

'Forget about the chung, then,' the Lama replied. 'But we
can still make love.'

He went inside, and she served him tea. Kunley offered
this grace:

'OM AH HUNG
This brew hasn't the faintest aroma of tea,
So how should we expect the smell of butter?
Nobody will drink this stuff –
I offer it to the wall!'

And he threw it on the floor. The girl smiled, and pulling his arm, she sang:

> 'This being has no smell of the mundane,
> Let alone the divine!
> Nobody will give him lodging,
> So I offer him a place outside the door!'

And she made as if to drag him out of the house, but her sexual needs overcame her.

Later that night, after she had gone to bed, Kunley got in beside her and thrust his Thunderbolt into her. She pretended not to feel it so he withdrew it and was about to leave her when she put her arms around him and drew him to her, so that he had no alternative but to take her.

The following morning he went down to the market place where all the villagers were gathered, and shouted out for them to hear, 'Gokye Palmo pretended to be asleep when I wanted her. But then when I tried to leave her, she wouldn't let me go!'

Then he left.

Gorphok Lama invited the Naljorpa to his home. 'My mother died last year,' he told the Lama. 'Would you please pray for her soul?'[7]

'Your unfortunate mother is imprisoned in that rock down there,' he told Gorphok Lama. Pointing to the rock, upon his command it began rolling up the hill towards them. He broke the rock open and out jumped a frog as big as a thumb. 'Go to the Pure Land of Delight,[8] old woman!' he told her, and from the frog's fontanelle a red syllable HRI emerged and vanished into the western sky.

This miracle was observed by many people, and that rock can still be seen preserved in the wall of the temple that was built there.

Moving on, the Lama came to the head of the Jelai La pass (between Wong Dzong and Tongsar), and while he was wondering whether he should descend through Mang Dewa to Khyen Yul, he met an old man with a heavy load. 'What is in your load?' he asked.

'Barley,' came the reply.

And the Lama thought, 'There's no prophecy concerning my coming here.' And then aloud, 'What villages will I find down in the valley?'

'First Rukhupee, then Chandanpee, and then Tangsepee,' the old man told him.

'I don't think that I will go to the valley of the three pee-pees,' he said, and returned the way he had come.

At Khyung Sekha he stayed with Mistress Gyaldzom. The girl served him liquor and chung, and sang him this song:

'Drukpa Kunley of Tibet!
Not only are you handsome and fair,
But you spread amazing grace.
In the rising, cooling spring breeze,
Is there any substance?
And in the descent of the River Tsangpo
Is there any obstruction?'

The Lama replied:

'Mistress Gyaldzom of Khyung Sekha!
Not only are you shapely and charming
But you are skilled in the pelvic upthrust.
If there is no substance
In the rising, cooling spring breeze,
On what, then, does the vulture glide?
And if there is no obstruction
In the falling River Tsangpo,
What, then, are mountains and boulders?
So, if there is no unreal fancy
In the mind of Drukpa Kunley,
What, then, is Mistress Gyaldzom?'

He made motions as if to leave, but Gyaldzom stopped him. 'You must eat before you go,' she said. 'I haven't cooked meat this evening, but I have some eggs.'

'I prefer chickens to their eggs,' said the Lama. 'Bring me a chicken!'

She cut off the chicken's head with a knife, and cooked and served the bird. When Kunley had finished eating he snapped his fingers at the pile of chicken's bones. 'Arise!' he commanded. The chicken pulled itself together, but one of

'. . . *straddling the valley with her breasts flying.* . . .'

its legs was missing. Gyaldzom found it in the pot. The Lama told her to take the one-legged chicken down to the river as it would be a bad omen to have about the house. One-legged chickens can still be seen in that area.

At the Phang Yul Monastery the Lama was met by some men of that place: 'We are patrons of Sakya Pandita,'[9] they told him. 'Spring has gone, our fields are dry, and there is no rain for our crops. Please perform a rain-making rite for us.'

'Tomorrow morning when the cock crows, climb high up on the valley side and make the sound of falling rain,' the Lama directed.

The next morning, the village headman did as the Lama had suggested, but he made the sound, 'Cho ro ro! Cho ro ro!'

'Akha kha!' Kunley exclaimed when the man returned. 'You should have said "Sha ra sha ra dung dung!" Now you will receive only a little rain.'

'This land cannot rise (shar shar) and the sound of the conch (dung) burns the ear,' said the headman. 'A little is sufficient.'

'Let there be no more rain in the summer than in the winter,' the Lama prayed. As a result of this rain making rite, there has been no excess of rainfall in the summer and no lack of it in the winter in Phang Yul until this day.

On the Dompa La pass the Lama looked out over the land of They and had a vision of an establishment of the Drukpa School founded on a hill that resembled the tip of an elephant's trunk.[10]

Then he had a premonition that the time was propitious to visit the Mystic Consort Adzom of Gomto and he set out to find her. On the way he stopped at Dar Wongkha (below Punakha) to transfer the consciousness of a dying man to the Plenum of Emptiness. Having done that he looked up and saw the Lady Adzom swaying her hips, tapping her feet, and singing, by the Stupa of Gomyul Sar. And he sang her this song:

'Looking up from Dar Wongkha
I see the Dakini of Gomyul Sar

Dancing by the Stupa like a goddess
And her name is Lady Adzom.
On the eighth day of the moon after midnight
Duty-Free Kunley will visit you.
Prepare me a little rice chung
And tinkle your cymbals, your sweet lips,
And sing me pleasant songs awhile
And let what follows, come naturally!
OM MANI PEME HUNG!'

At the appointed time Drukpa Kunley arrived at
Adzom's house and knocked on the door. The girl answered it, having neglected to tie her gown.

'Ah! You are ready and waiting for me,' he said. 'We
don't need an introduction.' And laying her on the doorstep, he made love to her. Afterwards she served him chung
and all sorts of good things, and he spent several days
engaged in drinking, playing, and enjoying Adzom. When
he was ready to leave, she besought him to stay with her
forever.

'Since your nether lotus is a tight bud, I'll return to you
for a further nine days,' he told her. 'And because you're an
artist in posture, another nine days, and another nine days
because you're good-hearted.' With that promise he left.

Descending from Drimthang he met a man of the Theb clan
accompanied by his wife. They invited him back to their
house praising his grace and blessing.

'Do you have any chung?' he asked.

'We have about five measures,' they told him.

So he went with them, and they told him their troubles.
'We had five sons but all of them died. Now we have
another young son, and we are afraid that he will follow his
brothers. We would be grateful if you would perform the
rite which binds the evil spirits that could afflict him.'

He told them to show him their son, and he immediately
saw that the boy was the phantom form of an elemental
ghost. He threw the boy into the river as he had done once
before to Samye Guardian. At first the parents wept and
wailed, but then they grew confident, and by and by they
asked the Lama for the blessing of another son.

'You must couple constantly,' he told them, 'and in

another year you will have another son. Call him Auspicious Increase.'

It is said that the Theb family of Drimthang are descended from that son.

The Lama decided to take a horse and ride to visit Namkha Dronma at Pachang near Lopaisa. On the way he again passed through the valley over which the Long Rong Demoness reigned. Out of jealousy she had broken the vow with which the Lama had bound her, and he found her straddling the valley with her breasts flying in the wind, her hair trailing on the ground, and her organ gaping between her thighs. As Drukpa Kunley approached she sang this song:

'A vagabond ascetic is descending the hill –
Is it the spiritual son of a clairvoyant Lama
Or a miracle working devil?
Is it a prattling madman
Or a drifter whose life ends where the road ends?
Anyway, it looks like Drukpa Kunley.
Where do you come from this morning?
You will not pass further along this road.
It's time for you to meditate, Holy Lama!
Time for you to pray to your horse!'

And showing him a most savage face, she turned the river back upstream. The Lama took hold of the shaft of his Thunderbolt with his right hand and raised it aloft, and with his left hand he grasped the Demoness's breasts:

'The snow lion, king of all beasts with claws,
Thrice skilled in the jungle lore, his body adorned with
       the turquoise mane –
He is without peer, fearless in the high snow mountains.
The tigress roaming in the southern, Sengdeng Jungle,
Courageous and cunning, her body covered in stripes –
She is the fearless empress of all beasts.
The fish-queen swimming in the western Maphamyu Lake,[11]
With iridescent scaly body –
She is fearless, unexcelled in the wind tossed waters.
This Divine Madman, Drukpa Kunley of Tibet,
His Body of the Four Joys[12] replete with bliss –

He is fearless in your vast vagina, Devil Woman.
Long Rong Demoness, Contented Protectress of Truth!
Last year in the first part of the night
You offered me your life essence,
And I appointed you Temple Guardian.
Now, shameless one, you dissimulate before me!
This morning I came from Tokmethang,
This evening I am going to Ronyom Monastery,
And here I will play in the Fountain of Truth![13]
Do not harm others
If you would not be harmed yourself!'

The Lama mounted his horse without hesitation and spurred it on, but the Demoness fled into a great boulder. The Lama thrust his Thunderbolt into the rock and said:

'Long Rong Demoness, Contented Protectress of Truth!
Never harm other living beings!
If in the future you wish mischief on anyone
I will destroy you as I destroy this rock!'

And he burst the rock into smithereens. It is still possible to see the pieces of this rock down by the Long Rong River. Suddenly a loud disembodied voice boomed:

'Drukpa Kunley, conqueror of your own mind!
I am the elemental consort you left behind.
When you opened yourself to human girls
I confess I was vengeful and jealous.
I beg you to be patient with me.'

Then she appeared in the centre of the river looking sad and repentant. She took a yak horn full of rice chung and offered it to the Lama gracefully, repeating her vow never to harm living beings. The Lama renamed her Happy Encounter, reappointing her Protectress of the Khyimed Temple.[14]

At Pachang Drukpa Kunley rested outside the house of the girl called Namkha Dronma and waited for her to appear. The girl saw him from a window, and although she had never set eyes upon him before, the very sight of him awoke her spiritual potential and she sang this song:

'Resplendent beggar resting on the ground,
Are you not Drukpa Kunga Legpa?

Please listen a moment to this maiden's song!
Noon-day sun at your zenith,
On whatever continent you shine
You never cast a shadow;
Stay with me here this morning
And give warmth and comfort quickly
To this clothless waif.
Master of the Treasury of Truth and Wealth,
Wherever you travel
You are never in need;
Stay in this land awhile
And bestow your wealth-power
On this poverty stricken mouse.
Drukpa Kunley, Master of Truth,
Wherever you wander abroad
You show impartial kindness;
Stay with me here in my house
And to this friendless virgin
Give perfect understanding.

The Lama was impressed with her intelligence, and knowing that she was a suitable candidate for initiation he gave her this reply:

'I am the sun at its zenith
And upon whatever continent I shine
I cast no shadow.
The comforting sun never penetrates
North facing caves,
So if your clothes are threadbare
Live in a cave facing east.
I am the Master of the Treasury of Plenty
And in whatever place I stay
It is true I am never in need,
But I am unable to give my power
To those without merit gained by giving.
So even though you are a penniless wretch
Give away all that you have.
I am the Duty-Free Drukpa Kunley
And in whatever land I roam
I live for the sake of others.
But I am unable to give realization
To those who have no devotion,
So if you wish to gain Buddhahood now
First show your faith and devotion.

Namkha Dronma served him tea, chung, and food. 'You are very beautiful, Namkha Dronma,' he told her. 'Aren't you married yet?'

'I am still a virgin,' she replied.

'Yah! Yah!' he said assuringly, 'We will do it slowly!'

Still drinking chung he took her inside. Before sitting down on the carpet he said, 'First the carpet must be consecrated. Lie down here!'

She shut the door. 'Will it be painful?' she asked.

'No, but if you have any butter, bring me a little.' He smeared a little butter on his Thunderbolt and then made love to her. 'Did it hurt?' he asked her when they had finished.

'I can't say whether it was pleasure or pain,' she replied, 'but I know that I feel better now than ever before.'

'What were you thinking?' he asked.

'I wasn't thinking anything,' she told him. 'I was just feeling!'

'That is how it should be,' he assured her. Then he gave her instruction on the Great Bliss of the Lower Door. He stayed with her several days, revealing the essence of the perspective of the most Profound Reality and then sent her to meditate in the mountains of the Hidden Valley of Pema Tsal,[15] telling her that he would visit her later.

On the way to Gahselok he met a woman with a heavy load. 'What are you carrying, mother?' he asked her.

'Tsampa,' she replied.

The Lama knew that there was no prophecy concerning her, but he asked her what villages lay beneath them.

'First Thohukha, then Masikha, then Changekha, and then Khatokha,' she replied.

'I'm not going to places with so many kha-s (mouths or apertures),' he said, and returned the way he had come.

In Naynying Lungpa he found a man building an irrigation dam whom he knew was threatened by death from a demoness that very night.

'What are you doing, father?' he asked.

'Can't you see! I'm building a dam,' said the old man.

'Where are you staying the night?'

'I'll stay here,' said the Lama. 'I'm tired of walking up and down. Do you have any chung?'

'If you can work hard I'll get you chung,' the old man offered.

'There's no work beyond me. Go and fetch the chung.' And the Lama stayed there in the field. At nightfall he lay down to sleep, and at midnight the demoness came and tried to drag him away by his feet. He took out his Flaming Thunderbolt, and she fled with the Lama in hot pursuit. Finally she vanished into a boulder around which Kunley built a wall. 'Come not forth until the end of the world,' he commanded. And he returned to the field.

When the old man returned the next morning the Lama had built the dam with his magical powers, according to the old man's needs. The old man was astounded and offered him chung. 'You are certainly no ordinary man,' he told the Lama. 'Are you not some ghost come to harm me?'

'Last night your real enemy came to kill you,' Kunley informed him, 'but I imprisoned her in a rock up on the valley side.'

The old man was filled with faith and prostrated to the Lama:

'I did not know my guest was a Buddha,
I had not realized he saved my life,
Or that he could build a dam by magic!
Please forgive me for all my ignorance.'

Thus he entered the Path of the Buddhas, his life was saved, his dam was built, and he had time to spare in which to practise meditation. What great benevolence had Drukpa Kunley!

Then, knowing that the time was ripe for Zangmo Chodzom, the Lama climbed over the Hing La pass and descended into Wong Barpaisa (in Thimpu district). He found the girl coming for water, and asked her if she had chung for him in the house and whether he could stay with her that night. She said she had both chung and a bed for him, and invited him inside where she plied him with chung, food, and tea, and finally, offered him a pot of liquor. He drank half of it. 'Now this saint has become quite intoxicated,' he told her, 'and his penis is hard. Are you a virgin, Chodzom? Answer me truthfully.'

'Well, when I was visiting Chunglay Gang last year, Khol Gok Sithar Paljor put his penis inside me, but I didn't feel it. That doesn't count, does it?'

'Just listen to me!' cried Kunley.

> 'Listen to my song, Zangmo Chodzom!
> You say you are a virgin
> Yet last year in Chunglay Gang
> This Khol Gok Sithar Paljor
> Pierced your Lotus with his Thunderbolt.
> What if not that is copulation?
> And what if not foreplay is kissing and hugging?
> Now it doesn't matter what you want –
> I desire no such leftovers as you!'

Chodzom knelt down on her knees before him and sang this entreaty:

> 'O Naljorpa, do not be angry!
> Please listen to this song I sing!
> The midnight moon above
> Never hears the Dragon Planet's approach[16]
> Until too late – it is swallowed up.
> But it always reappears unblemished.
>
> 'The garden flower below
> Never knows when the frost is coming
> Until it begins to wither and die.
> But always it blooms the next year.
>
> 'This self-willed girl
> Had no desire for men like Kholkho,
> Yet she was quite powerless to resist him.
> But now surely the taint has gone.
>
> 'Naljorpa, you take the good with the bad,
> Please accept this gift of my body.'

The Lama sang this in reply:

> 'It is true that the midnight moon above
> Cannot anticipate the Dragon Planet's coming,
> And after powerlessly accepting its eclipse
> It always appears brightly shining.

'And it's true that the garden flower below
Cannot anticipate frost and hail,
And although it helplessly withers
It revives in succeeding years.

'You fortunate girl of good birth,
It is true that you had no desire for Kholkho
And were helpless to resist his advances –
You won't be deprived of future pleasure!'

'Will you make love to me if I purify myself with water and incense?' she begged him. The Lama assented, and after she had washed and purified herself in the smoke of incense, he took her. While he was still engaged with her, a child wandered into the room.

'Look! A child's here!' she whispered urgently.

'I told you the time wasn't right,' he said. 'You didn't listen, and now it doesn't matter if his parents come too, I'll not stop!' And he continued his work.

The children brought their parents and a crowd gathered. The girl tried to make him stop. 'I don't care how many people or demons watch,' he said, 'I'll not be interrupted.'

'Look at that shameless couple!' people said.

'I'm not humping my mother!' Kunley told them. 'Why be shocked? If you don't know how to do it, now's the time to learn.' And he continued to the end.

Chodzom was so ashamed that her former guilt was washed away, and she became one of the lucky ones.

The Lama heard that the abbot Ngawong Chogyal had come to visit the South from Ralung, and he went to meet him. On the way he visited his son Tsewong Tenzin and his wife Palzang Buti at Chakdar.[17] There he entered into the Mandala of Smiles and Laughter, and his family flourished and increased.

8 How Drukpa Kunley returned from Bhutan to Tibet and the Events which attended his Nirvana

We bow to the Lord of Beings, Choje Drukpa Kunga Legpa,
Bearer of the Shield of Loving Kindness, Compassion
   and Patience,
Leader of a hunting dog that destroys the five poisons,[1]
Possessor of the bow and arrow that unifies Insight and
   Skilful Means in Emptiness.

Then the Master of Truth, Lord of Beings, Kunga Legpa, went to Punakha, to the jewel crest of the mountain shaped like an elephant's trunk, which nowadays is called Jilli Gang. There he was greeted by the abbot Ngawong Chogyal, who had been invited to the Southerners' Homeland by the elders. After he had exchanged courtesies with the abbot, whose attendants prostrated before him, they went inside and remained closeted for some time, exchanging personal news. Before leaving, Drukpa Kunley told Ngawong Chogyal that he would go to visit his Mystic Consort Adzom, but that he would return the next day in time to bestow the ambrosia at the abbot's Rite of Empowerment.[2]

The following day, as the abbot sat enthroned in the market place before a vast throng of devotees, the Lama arrived carrying his bow and arrows, his sleek hunting dog on one side of him, and the Lady Adzom, dressed in her flashing ornaments, on his left arm. The assembly was stunned.

'The Flask of Ambrosia[3] is not needed today,' he told the abbot, who was in the process of consecrating the vessel. 'I will provide the nectar myself. Each of you close your eyes and stretch out your hands to receive it.' Then holding his penis in his right hand he passed a drop of urine into each of the outstretched hands. Some partook with devotion, taking refuge as they did so, finding the liquid to be sweet. Others spat it out, crying that it was urine, and wiping their hands. Those who drank with reverence gained power and realization, while those who spat it out gained only a run of bad luck. Even today water is scarce in Jili Gang.

The abbot continued with the rite and Kunley wandered around the market place hand in hand with the Lady Adzom, squeezing her breasts, kissing her, laughing and playing, doing whatever came into his head. Then a man called Sithar Gyalpo arose from his seat in the crowd. 'Things like that should be done at night when no one can see,' he told the Lama. 'Nevertheless, nothing you can do can destroy our faith in you or destroy our concentration. Please do not leave the market place without granting us a blessing of the MANI PEME.'

'Certainly I will bless you,' said the Lama and sang this song:

'OM MANI PEME HUNG
People say Drukpa Kunley is utterly mad –
In madness all sensory forms are the Path!
People say that Drukpa Kunley's organ is immense –
His member brings joy to the hearts of young girls!
People say that Drukpa Kunley is too fond of sex –
Congress results in a host of fine sons!
People say that Drukpa Kunley has an amazing, tight arse –
A tight arse shortens the rope of Samsara!
People say that Drukpa Kunley has a bright red vein –
A red vein gathers a cloud of Dakinis!
People say that Drukpa Kunley does nothing but babble –
This babbler has forsaken his homeland!
People say that Drukpa Kunley is extraordinarily handsome –
His beauty endears him to the Mon girls' hearts!
People say that Drukpa Kunley is verily a Buddha –
Through subjection of the enemy of ignorance, awareness grows!

And the marketplace was filled with undivided faith.

That night the Lama was looking deep within his own mind to discover where best his offspring might flourish, when

he saw a vision of a thousand Fire Spirits gathered on top of
the high mountain peak above him. Immediately he picked
a blazing brand out of the fire and threw it into the middle of
the demonic host. The entire valley was filled with the smell
of burning flesh. The Lama then transported himself to the
mountain top and built a small stupa to contain the malevolent forces of that area. The stick which he had thrown from
below grew into a tree which is said to be the axis of the old
Karchi Stupa.

The following day Ngawong Chogyal summoned him
to his room. 'You stay with me here and yet you harm other
creatures,' he told the Lama indignantly. 'Last night I
distinctly smelt roast pork. Please leave this place.'

'Do not be angry,' Kunley replied. 'Listen to this song.'

> 'While I was divining a home for my children,
> Seeking signs and portents last night,
> Looking up at the mountain peak,
> I saw a thousand Fire Elementals.
> As soon as I saw them, I destroyed them,
> But I could not prevent the smell of burnt flesh.
>
> 'Peering up at a house's eves,
> A fungus is clinging to a beam –
> Even a violent wind will not loosen it.
> Peering up a long leg,
> A clit is clinging to a beaver –
> Even an arrogant penis will not loosen it.
>
> 'The people of the east are strongmen and heroes,
> The people of the south wear clothes of leaves,
> The people of the west are mother-humpers,
> And the people of the north are gourmets.
>
> 'There is good chung at the bottom of the pail
> And happiness lies below the navel!'

The abbot was somewhat mollified by the Lama's verses,
but nevertheless he said, 'I have received an invitation to go
to Gomto tomorrow and if you are going to behave badly, I
don't want you following me. You will pervert my faithful
patrons' minds and shame me.'

The following morning Drukpa Kunley left for Gomto

before the abbot. Arriving in the marketplace, he found a large crowd gathered, waiting for Ngawong Chogyal with tea and chung. In response to their queries he told them that the abbot was on his way, and then he climbed upon the throne that had been set up for the abbot and started to entertain the crowd with mimicry and jokes. The abbot found him still entertaining when he arrived.

'I told you not to come here today,' he reprimanded. 'Why did you disobey me?'

'You told me not to follow you,' Kunley laughed. 'You didn't tell me not to come at all.'

'Then I expect you to behave and not to play the fool,' said the abbot. 'Now please make an offering of the chung.'

So holding a bowl of chung in his hand, the Lama delivered this offering and intercession:[4]

'Accept this offering, Great Vajra Bearer,
May you empty Samsara of suffering.
Accept this offering, Tilopa,
And show us the nature of our minds.
Accept this offering, Pandita Naropa,
And clear the way of the messenger.
Accept this offering, Translator Marpa,
And give us understanding of the Lama's Secret Teaching.
Accept this offering, Milarepa,
Give us rebirth in a family free from want.
Accept this offering, Ngawong Chogyal,
And let us be able to renounce our homeland.
Accept this offering, Professors of Logic,
And may the apt word arise in debate.
Accept this offering, Lamas of small monasteries,
May selfish, petty disputes be settled amicably.
Accept this offering, Gomchens and Naljorpas,
May you break the hip bones of nuns.
Accept this offering, girls of the market place,
May your sex bring you food and clothing.
Accept this offering, Drukpa Kunley,
May you carry your wealth on your penis head!'

'Now drink your chung and begone,' said the abbot when the Lama had finished. 'Don't stay around my initiation ceremony.'

'All right' said Kunley. 'Your priestcraft earns you the

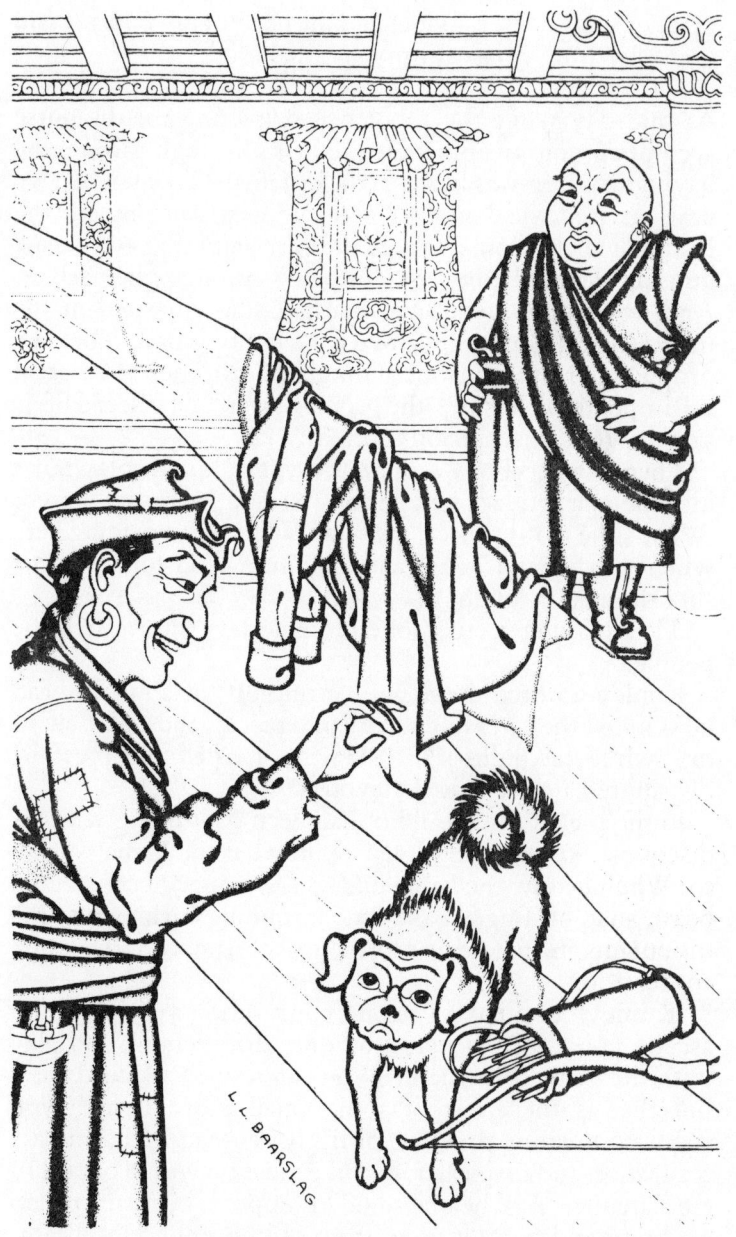

'*The Lama hung his bow and arrows, and his dog, on a sunbeam.*'

price of your horses' fodder and the price of my pussy. I will go to Adzom's house for my spiritual food.'

At mid-day while the abbot was delivering the discourse accompanying his initiation rite from his high throne, the baying of a dog was heard in the distance. 'Today when we have invited the Lama to give us deep teaching on the Buddhas' Path, some wicked men are gathering evil karma hunting deer,' the people whispered amongst themselves. And at that moment an exhausted stag appeared in the marketplace, closely followed by a hunting dog. The deer dropped to rest at the foot of the abbot's throne. 'How great is Rimpoche's blessing!' the people purred. 'The deer's life is saved. What an auspicious portent!'

Then to everybody's amazement, Drukpa Kunley burst into the marketplace with his bow strung, an arrow poised. 'What's the matter, deer?' he said. 'What are you doing here when you should be up and running?' And forthwith he shot the stag through.

'He's playing a cruel joke on us today,' murmured the people.

Kunley ignored them, and cutting off the animal's head he skinned the carcass, cut it up into pieces, and laid it out to dry while he built a fire. Having roasted the meat he distributed a piece to each devotee.

In the meantime the abbot had been continuing with his discourse, keeping an eagle eye on what the Lama was up to. When he saw the Lama pile up the stripped bones of the beast, snap his fingers, and send it running back up into the mountains, he felt he was losing too much face and became contentious.

'Kunley! You have a strong constitution yet you do no ascetic yoga whatsoever. You only drink chung and play with the girls. It is true that you can resurrect a dead deer, but that is the effect of some small power which you acquired in some previous birth. If you had both ultimate realization and magical power like me, you would be able to emulate me.' And he unwound his upper robe from around his body and hung it up in front of him upon a sunbeam. However, the sunbeam bent slightly under its weight.

The Lama laughed. 'You jerk off!' he said. 'It is truly miraculous that someone like you, a puppet on a high throne burdened with the weight of others' minds, can perform a trick like that. But this is the proper way to do it.' The Lama proceeded to hang his bow and arrow, and his dog, on a sunbeam. The sunbeam remained taut.

'Why does this sunbeam bend when it has only a robe hanging on it, when your sunbeam remains taut with a dog on it?' asked the puzzled abbot.

'Our degree of spiritual realization and detachment is the same,' Kunley told him. 'But the weight of your possessions and material comforts makes your magic heavier. I have a higher vision.'

In spite of themselves, the assembly was deeply impressed and sighed with devotion. 'This Lama is Palden Drukpa himself!' they said. 'Ngawong Chogyal has a vast power of blessing, but Drukpa Kunley is a Naljorpa unparalleled and peerless.' And Drukpa Kunley's fame spread throughout the South, and later through U and Tsang in Tibet.

One day Ngawong Chogyal said to Drukpa Kunley, 'Spring is here. It is becoming hot. We two should return to Tibet.'

'Go if you must,' replied the Lama. 'But the valley girls' bottoms keep me here. However, I don't think I will be delayed more than a year. This old bird begins to yawn, tired of roaming, and when I finally return my spirit will break.' He accompanied the abbot for some distance, and then, bowing his head, received his blessing.

Ngawong Chogyal returned through Paro to his monastery at Ralung, while Drukpa Kunley stayed with his Mystic Consort Adzom.

Walking above Samdingkha one day, he encountered a group of workmen digging irrigation ditches and thought he should help to bring water to the dry fields of that area.

'You need chung when you do this kind of work,' said the Lama.

'We have none,' they answered.

'I will stay here, and if you bring chung I will help you

with your work,' the Lama offered.

'Do whatever you please,' they told him, 'it doesn't matter to us.'

The Lama saw that there was no auspicious omen there. 'Let the people of this place depend upon rainwater for ever,' he prayed. Until this day the fields behind Drakwok Nang have never been irrigated.

In Drakwok Nang (in Pungthang district) the Lama stayed with Apa Tashi and Ama Nanga Lhamo. 'We are most honoured to have you in our house today,' the couple told him. 'Please stay and be our daughter's husband.'

'If I'm going to marry your daughter I need chung,' said the Lama.

They brought him seven measures of chung and he began drinking. 'The chung is first class,' he opined, 'I will pay you well for it.' And he transformed the boiled grain from which the chung had been pressed into gold.

Later when Apa was about to go out to cut a tree to replace a pillar in the house, the Lama offered to do the work for him. 'I am used to erecting pillars!' he said. With his magic he immediately erected a solid pillar which two men could barely have carried.

He also performed a Rite of Water Divination, and the spring which he discovered beside Apa Tashi's field remains to this day.

He travelled on, passing through Gomyul Sar (in Garsa district) where he stopped to visit the Lady Adzom and to give her the advice that she needed. Then going down the valley from Khawa Chara (in Pungthang district), he found some boys fishing, and asked them for a fish.

'You have nothing to do,' they said, 'hook one yourself.'

Suddenly the venomous serpent-demon that lived in a large black rock above the river appeared before them in the stream in the form of a fish ogre.

'You serpent-demon! Even if you turn into a giant yoni ogre you won't scare me!' he shouted at it. And catching it with his hand he dashed it upon a rock, leaving an imprint that can still be seen today.

The demon returned to its original savage form and was immediately assaulted by the Lama's Flaming Thunderbolt of Wisdom. After it vanished into the rock, the Lama extracted a vow of obedience and non-violence from it before building a small Stupa upon the rock. At a later date a devout layman built a small temple called the Temple of the Fish around the Stupa.

Finally, the Lama sang this song:

> 'This Khawa Chara Tsekhar
> Is a land which lives on fish.
> Reject the small fish
> And kill at once the large fish you catch.'

At Khawa Ngoshing the Lama found a flat flailing stone and inscribed these words upon it with his finger: 'Men pass to and fro together, but I have no companion, and my heart is sad. If I leave this Khawa Ngoshing, no one will try to prevent me, and if I stay, no one will tell me it is better to leave. I will travel on regardless.'

Then he thought he would go to visit his wife and son. On the way he met some travellers who asked where he was bound from the land of They.

The Lama replied:

> 'The spring has come
> And the eltok flower is blooming.
> It's time to drink the best chung,
> Time for this small Tibetan to go home,
> And time to visit Palzang Buti.'

He left them on the road and went to Chakdar, in the Highlands, to visit his wife and son for the last time. He stayed there for some days teaching them the true ways of the Inner Doctrine and imbuing them with pure aspiration.

At Chang Gang Kha (in Thimpu district) he decided to perform a Rite of Protection for his devout patron, Lama Paljor, to prevent him falling off the path. Arriving at Lama Paljor's house he found the Lama within with his four concubines, and yet another ravishing girl at the centre of a dispute. The Lama Paljor had abducted the girl from her

family, and her relatives had found her, and now stood with
drawn swords about to murder her abductor.

'Don't fight over a woman!' cried Kunley. 'Listen to this
story.'

A long time ago in India in a kingdom called Nagrota
ruled by a powerful and wealthy raja called Paladha, lived
two men named Bhasu and Dhasu. These two men were
alike in wealth, taste and reputation, and before their god,
Mahadev, they had sworn an oath of fidelity to one another.
Bhasu had an extremely beautiful wife whom Dhasu
coveted. He justified this by telling himself that the oath
which he had sworn with Bhasu was invalid since Bhasu
possessed something he could not share. In order to deceive
his friend he went to him with a thousand gold pieces and
spun this story.

'I am going on an extended business trip,' he told Bhasu.
'Please keep this money until I return.'

'We should have a witness to this transaction,' Bhasu's
wife suggested, and she invited the Rishi, Dhara, whose
honesty was unquestionable, to be witness. The gold passed
hands and Dhasu departed.

After a year had gone by, Dhasu returned one night and
asked Bhasu's wife for his gold.

'We should fetch the witness,' said the woman.

'Why bother?' said Dhasu. 'It's my own gold.'

She acquiesced, and returned the gold to him.

Six months later he went to Bhasu's house again. 'How
are you both?' he asked. 'My business has not been so good
and I need my gold. Please accept this horse as a gift in
return for your kindness.'

'What are you saying?' said Bhasu astonished. 'You've
already taken back your gold. You can't have it twice.
Come in and have a drink and rest for a while. We should
stay friends at least, but I cannot accept your horse, thank
you.'

'If you don't have my gold, I'm certainly not going to
drink with you,' said Dhasu. 'I came for my gold and our
friendship is at an end if I don't get it. But why should we
quarrel. I will fetch the witness Dhara to settle the matter.'

The Rishi arrived and averred that he had not seen the

gold since the original transaction.

Then the three of them went to the king for a settlement. The king's judgment found Bhasu guilty, for the Rishi and Dhasu showed agreement in that the gold had never been returned.

'You have stolen another man's money,' said the king in judgment. 'You have tried to deceive me and my ministers, and you have cast aspersions on the Rishi's honesty. I sentence you to give your beautiful wife to the man whose gold you stole, and you yourself will face death by burning.'

A wood and tar tax was levied from the townspeople, a fire was lit, and Bhasu was cast into the flames.

'I can never be your wife,' cried Bhasu's wife to Dhasu. 'Your gold was returned and you know it. And now my innocent husband is being burnt alive. Please let me express myself sincerely for the sake of our old friendship.'

> 'The wedge of karma is very thin
> And even saints can face disaster.
> Destroyed by dependence upon a dishonest friend,
> Cheated by a friend's broken pledge,
> My husband is burnt, and my eyes fill with tears.
> If I could ever betray my husband's memory
> My mind is surely deluded!'

With these words she threw herself into the flames with her husband. That is the origin of the custom of Suttee which is practised in India and Nepal to this day.[5]

Not long after, Dhasu died of melancholia, his evil designs having failed to gain his mean ambition. Thus Dhasu, Bhasu, and his wife found themselves together in the court of Dharmaraj, Lord of Death and Judge of Karma.

'Bhasu, you and your wife will be reborn as son and daughter of the Raja Paladha. You, Bhasu, will be reborn as the son of a swineherd who lives close to the palace,' judged Dharmaraj. And so it was.

The prince and princess grew to be very beautiful children but the swineherd's son was born with no mouth. 'What did the boy do in his last life that he should be born with eyes, ears, and a nose, but with no mouth?' wailed his mother. 'He sees others eating, feels hungry, and beats upon the food with his hands and feet, but how can he eat without a mouth?'

When Buddha passed by on his begging round, the mother took her son to him and laid him at his feet. 'O Omniscient One! Please tell me what unfortunate karma has caused this miserable birth,' she begged.

'Bring the king's son and daughter here,' directed the Buddha. When they arrived, Buddha recounted the story of their past lives in detail, and all three of them, remembering those events, wept together. Dhasu threw himself at Buddha's feet, weeping and wailing. The Lord shaved the head of the miserable boy, gave him the name Pure Joy, and ordained him as a lay devotee. He was sustained by burnt tsampa smoke. Buddha promised that he would finally gain Buddhahood.

'And that is the karma that hounds a man who blatantly steals another man's wife,' Drukpa Kunley told his audience.

Lama Paljor gave up all thought of taking the girl. 'O Drukpa Kunley, you always speak the truth! Please sing us a song of the South today.'

The Lama sang this song of the girls he had known:

> 'Tibetan teacher from Ralung,
> Your respectable family is not enough –
> What about powerful bliss-waves?
> Eltok flower of the snowlands,
> Your delicate colour is not enough –
> Where is your honey comb?
> Mistress Gyaldzom of Khyung Sekha,
> Your beautiful lotus is not enough –
> Where is your skill in the pelvic thrust?
> Lady Adzom of Gomto,
> Your attractive body is not enough –
> What about skill and style in bed?
> Paldzom Buti of Nyamo,
> Your skill in milking is not enough –
> What about kissing and foreplay?
> Gyengling Nyishar in Zhungyul,
> Your great faith is certainly not enough –
> Where is your thick rice chung?

> Gyalchok and Gyaldzom of Drung Drung,
> Unable to maintain your present situation
> What use is a broad mind to you?
> All scholars and laymen of the South,
> Why not drink thick rice chung,
> Instead of stealing calves' food?
> For Duty-Free Kunley, Master of Truth,
> Travelling abroad is not enough –
> What he needs is many consorts!
> Lama Paljor of Gang Kha,
> You could fulfil a desire for five score girls –
> Why quarrel over one?'

Lama Paljor was filled with reverence and devotion, and receiving the advice he needed, he thanked the Lama profoundly.

At Wong Barpaisa Drukpa Kunley stayed with Chodzom for several days. Then advising her to keep her mind centred in Nirvana, he bade her farewell. That night he arrived at Wong Gomtseugang and consulted the omens to divine whether or not it would be propitious to build a monastery there.

'Lama Buddha!' he called up from outside the temple.

'There's no Lama Buddha here,' answered the temple keeper, thinking that the Lama was calling someone by that name.

'Sacred Word!' called the Lama again, and received the same reply.

'Steward Wealth!' the Lama called finally, and again the reply was negative.

In his way he divined that the omens were unpropitious.

> 'There is grass on the upper, snow covered slopes,
> But here is insufficient grass for a goat;
> There's a river at the base of the mountain,
> But here is insufficient water to satisfy a bird;
> The mountain slopes are covered with forest,
> But here is insufficient wood to light a fire –
> You, Temple Keeper, are Master of the Three Zeros!'

As he was about to leave that place, he thought that at least he should make a small offering to the Lord. So he stuck his thumb into the earth and brought forth a spring.

At Tsalunang the Lama discovered that all the men-folk had gone to Wong to mine iron ore and that he was without a lodging. However, a devout woman called Dondrub Zangmo invited him to stay at her house.

'Have you any chung?' he asked her.

'I have seven measures,' she replied.

He went to her house and began drinking in her parlour. 'Do you have any miners in your household?' he asked suddenly.

'My twenty-three year old son, Tsering Wangyay, is down the pit,' she told him.

'Then put your lips to that empty Chinese clay pot and call his name,' he directed.

She did as she was told, and her son, hearing his name called in the pit at Wong, left his work and went above to see who called him. Just as he reached the surface a tunnel collapsed below, and twenty-nine men were buried alive.

Tsering Wangyay hurried home. 'Did you call my name?' he asked his mother.

'Yes, I called you,' his mother said. 'Where are your friends?'

'They were all buried down in the pit,' he told her.

'You have given me chung and hospitality, and this is a small measure of my gratitude,' the Lama told Dondrub Zangmo.

'If I had horses and elephants besides, I would certainly offer them to you!' she said joyfully, thanking him profusely.

In the upper part of the Tsalunang Valley he asked the whereabouts of Namkha Dronma. He found her in deep meditation in an inaccessible cave.

'O Namkha Dronma, how is it going?' he asked. She immediately arose and touched his feet with her forehead. 'When you have devotion as great as Buddha Sakyamuni, you will find your way out of the ravines of meditation and achieve a state of non-meditation,' he told her. 'Through the conjunction of the Lama's blessing and your own devotion, your finite mind will unite with the latent Buddha's mind within you, and you will gain a Body of Clear Light.'

On the fifteenth day of the first month she gained liberation of Sound, Light and Thought. It is said that even today on the fifteenth day of the first month, the Sound of Reality reverberates in that cave.

On Jelai La pass, which is called Jading Kha these days, the Lama came upon a large house in which he found people drinking dried radish soup which, however, they called meat soup. 'I feel the presence of the Fiend of Death,' the Lama told them. 'I am leaving.'

'Leave if you wish,' they replied. 'We are not superstitious.'

As soon as he was outside, the house collapsed, killing them all.

From the top of the Jel La pass (between Thimphu and Paro), the Lama looked down on the house of the Master Nyida Drakpa and thought that he should initiate the Master's daughter, Samten Tsemo of Paro. But when he arrived at the house he found that she had been betrothed and that the Master was teaching his own doctrine. Drukpa Kunley took these to be bad omens and sang this song:

'Up in the happy highland meadows,
Where a hundred yaks in a thousand are favoured,
The yak cow with unlucky karma was taken by traders
And deprived of her avaricious master –
Yak cow in the hands of meat-eaters!
Down below, there in the pure, blue river waters,
Where a hundred fish in a thousand are favoured,
The fish with unlucky karma was hooked by fishermen
And deprived of the waves of the pure, blue river –
Little fish in the hands of hungry men!
In the Tsang Tsing jungle of southern Bhutan,
Where a hundred birds in a thousand are favoured,
The tiny bird with unlucky karma was seized by a child
Unable to fly into the sky with its untrained wings –
Small bird in the hands of thoughtless children!
In this land, in Paro in Bhutan,

Where a hundred men in a thousand are favoured,
Sinful men were accepted into the Lama's monastery,
Deprived of their chance to absorb the Sacred Teaching –
Pity the mean Master and disciples breaking their vows in
    confusion.

The Master and his disciples were offended by the Lama's
insinuations and refused to offer him food or hospitality.
Seeing, also, that there was no auspicious omen concerning
the girl, Samten Tsemo, he decided that his work of conversion and subjugation in the South was completed and that
he should return immediately to Tibet. And so, by the
power of his concentration, he transported himself by
magic, and straightway found himself in his homeland.

There he met the abbot Ngawong Chogyal. 'O Kunga
Legpa, you know the old saying, "Old men don't travel
abroad." You should stay in one place. We can offer you
everything to support life here. And if that is not enough,
the gods and protectors will be at your disposal to provide
your requirements. Since you are master of the Celestial
Treasury of Every Desire, you need have no anxiety.'

Accepting the abbot's offer, Drukpa Kunley remained
for some time in the deep Samadhi of Immutable Heart
SAMAYA in the Glorious White Incense Chamber.

Afterwards, when he had been invited by some devout
patrons to Nangkatse, his diseased right foot dissolved into
rainbow light. This miracle was seen by all. Interpreting
this as a sign of his approaching Final Ecstasy, he went and
stayed with his son, Palden Zhingkyong Drukda, in the
monastery of Lamphar in Tolung.[6]

Thus it was that the Master of Truth, Lord of Beings,
Kunga Legpa, spent his days travelling throughout U and
Tsang, Ngari and Dokha, Jayul and Dakpo, Kongpo and
Bhutan, selflessly doing what was necessary to teach and
transform, taming the spirits of the land, bringing water to
the desert, wealth to the poor, sons to childless women,
knowledge to the ignorant, and showing the path to the
aimless. Such deeds of a Buddha involving extrasensory
powers, indeed, his entire life's work, cannot be expressed
in words, and his death, as his life, was associated with

events that are beyond the scope of our vision to compre-
hend on this side of Nirvana. Like the Buddha Munindra
(Sakyamuni), who, after a thorn had pricked his foot in the
acacia garden, exhibited slight physical indisposition as a
sign exhorting human beings to follow his teaching, this
Divine also affected sickness after he had concluded that his
work of transformation was completed. At the age of one
hundred and fifteen years, in the year of the iron horse (1570
AD), on the first day of the first month, he revealed his Final
Ecstasy. Perpetuating his reputation for equivocal activity,
his 'One Hundred Thousand Precepts' is not precise about
his age, but he is reputed to have lived one hundred and
fifteen years.

Earthquake, thunder, and lightning attended his passing
together with other auspicious signs which it is unnecessary
to describe. Thinking that he would provide a significant
portent that would perpetuate his message to mankind, he
did not dissolve his body completely, but left it behind in
the human realm in the form of strikingly powerful minia-
ture images of Sakyamuni, the Bodhisattva of Compassion,
the Saviouress, Jowo Atisha, the Deities Horse Neck and
Supreme Delight, and other Buddhas. He also left a vast
quantity of Ringsel.[7] The images and Ringsel were kept in
the treasury of the Tolung Lamphar Monastery, where
devout and fortunate pilgrims could view them, until
Zhabs-drung Rimpoche[8] visited the monastery and trans-
ferred the relics to the treasury of the Central Government
of Bhutan, where they remain today.

Benedictory Prayers

PRAYER OF GOOD WISHES

May this biography, this sun of compassionate grace,
This legend of Kunga Legpa of old –
A saint exalted in lineage, empowered by Truth –
Give us the pleasure of knowing the Lama personally.
As the gods above grow happy hearing it,
May they grant us our desires and pleasures.
As the serpents below grow happy hearing it,
May they grant us rain in due season.
As the guardian demons of this earth grow happy hearing it,
May they grant us speedy fulfilment of our ambitions.
And as the entire world grows happy hearing it,
May our crops be always abundant and may our cattle
    multiply.
And as malevolent spirits soften as they hear it,
May our troubles and difficulties be averted.
When our lust is excited as we read it,
May we enjoy the favours of attractive maidens.
When our pride of youth is aroused as we read it,
May we enjoy the strength of goat-horn penis heads.
When old women grow sad as they read it,
May they gain pleasure from a well-placed radish.
When young boys grow excited as they read it,
May they gain their heart's desire.
When the people's misery is relieved by hearing it,
May all beings of the Three Worlds be happy.
When the Final Goal is achieved by hearing it,
May all beings gain Buddhahood.

PRAYER OF GOOD LUCK

Some men prefer the blissful spaces of the heavens,
Some men prefer the wealth of the nether regions –
Good luck to gods and serpents!
Some men enjoy the pleasure of virtue,
Some men enjoy the wealth of kings –
Good luck to happy saints and miserable kings!
Ngawong Chogyal likes horses
Drukpa Kunley likes pussies –
Good luck to horse lover and pussy lover!
The disciple Legshe likes chung,
Palzang Dorje likes meat –
Good luck to chung drinker and meat eater!
Dzob Dzob Kharal enjoys playing dice,
While Azhang Khyung Kyab enjoys singing songs –
Good luck to gambler and singer!
Baleb Zung Zung enjoys reciting MANI PEME,
Dondrub Palzang likes fish –
Good luck to Dharma lover and fish lover!
Ani Atsun is happy lying down,
Apa Akyab is happy standing up –
Good luck to the passive and the active!
Topa Tsewong is happy in religion,
Duty-Free Kunley is happy in his hostess –
Good luck to religion lover and woman lover!
Tsunchung Tashi is happy in Tibet,
Tsondrup Zangpo is happy in the South –
Good luck to lovers of Tibet and Bhutan!
Young men drink chung with a hero's strength,
And wear fine clothes and jewelled rings –
Good luck to the spirit of youth!
Girls dress in silks and eat sweet foods,
Enjoying sex and bearing sons –
Good luck to maidens and women!
The Teaching's meaning and the listener's ear,
Study's import and the path which is practised –
Good luck to teachers and students!
Brothers in striving (the Sangha), the Path manifest (the
    Dharma),

And the Goal to be won (Buddha) –
May we be blessed by the Three Jewels!

DEDICATION OF MERIT

Stories of yesterday's adventures,
And even tales of the accomplishments of great saints
Whose actions are unfathomable, sound ridiculous
When recounted today without confidence and authority.
However, by virtue of the precious Golden Spoon, the
 Sacred Teaching,
Having opened the mind's eye a fraction, and by virtue of
 that alone,
Reading innumerable accounts of the Adept's life,
Every drop of the elixir of miraculous truth can be
 absorbed.
And, further, after distilling the essence of that elixir,
When the white conch-heart is saturated in purity
The Path of Knowledge can be inscribed with the kusha
 grass pen.
And this gift of relaxation to zealous minds
Can be despensed into every outstretched hand of faith and
 devotion
As an offering that gives to each his own joy.
And may the gentle stream of gathering virtue that arises
 from this offering,
Finally carry all beings into the Ocean of Omniscience.

Translator's Notes

Prologue, and Chapter One (pages 35-52)

1 Saraha, an arrowsmith, and his spiritual son, Shavaripa, a hunter, practised the Yoga of Spontaneity (*sahaja*) in India during the eighth and ninth centuries. Their songs (*caryapada*) show disdain for ritual worship and academic scholasticism, exalting an uninhibited, spontaneous effusion of divine word and action.

2 The world of confusion and suffering (*samsara*), and escape from the round of transmigration into its peaceful essence (*nirvana*), are ultimately identical: this is the Buddhas' realization.

3 The Sutras are the exoteric precepts of Sakyamuni Buddha, and the Tantras contain the secret liturgies, rites, and instructions, of Tantric practice.

4 rNal-'byor-pa, yogin: an itinerant mystic, Tantric Adept and meditator.

5 Narotapa or Naropa (1016-1100) was notable for his long and arduous search for his Guru, Tilopa, for the extremes of anguish to which his Guru subjected him, and the purity and power of his Mahamudra practice. He was the teacher of Marpa (the Tibetan Translator), and Atisha, and he formulated Naropa's Six Yogas.

6 Padmapani, the Protector of Tibet, is a form of Avalokitesvara, the Bodhisattva of Compassion, who stands holding a white lotus. Both supernal and incarnate Bodhisattvas are emanations of a Buddha, living in Samsara to teach and assist all sentient beings.

7 The Gya family of the province of Tsang are an ancient Tibetan clan.

8 Palden Drukpa Rimpoche, Yeshe Dorje (1161-1211), founded the Drukpa Kahgyu School at Ralung in East Tsang. He was a disciple of Pema Dorje (Lingrepa) and Phakmotrupa.

9 Each year of the sixty year cycle of the Tibetan calendar, commencing in 1026 AD, is denominated by one of the five Chinese elements, one of the twelve beasts, and as either male or female. In addition each year has a name such as 'The Royal Bull'.

10 'Master of Truth' (*chos-rje*) implies a Buddha's attainment, and Kunga Legpai Zangpo (*Kun-dga' legs-pa'i bzang-po*) is the full form of Kunley (*Kun-legs*) or Kunga Legpa. 'Drukpa' is an indicator of his school, the Drukpa Kahgyu, and not that he belongs to Bhutan (*Druk*). Drukpa means 'The Dragon'.

11　The Three Secret Teachings (*gdam-sngags sdong-pe gsum*) refer to oral instructions upon the spontaneous purification of body, speech, and mind.

12　The Four Initiations and Empowerments (*dbang-bskur bzhi*), the Vase, Secret, Wisdom, and Word Empowerments, consecrate the initiate as the Deity in whose name the rite is performed, and confer the power to practise the grades of Creation and Fulfilment associated with the Deity. A distinction is made here between the external, formal empowerment and the real inner meaning.

13　The Three Vows (*sdom-pa gsum*) are the *Hinayana* vow of strict moral and physical discipline, the *Mahayana* Bodhisattva Vow to act always to benefit others, and the *Vajrayana* Tantric Vow to maintain constant spiritual union (SAMAYA) with the Buddha Lama, and subsidiary vows.

14　The Teaching (*dharma, chos*) refers to the entire corpus of instruction upon the methods of escaping the cycle of transmigration and attaining Buddhahood.

15　Ralung is half way between Lhasa and the Bhutan border; it is the seat of the Drukpa Kahgyupas, the homeland of the Gya Clan, and close to Drukpa Kunley's birthplace. See map, Appendix I.

16　Ngawong Chogyal (*Ngag-dbang chos-rgyal*) 1465–1540, a scion of the Gya Clan, possibly a cousin of Drukpa Kunley, and abbot of the Ralung Monastery, who made several evangelical pilgrimages to Bhutan, is Drukpa Kunley's fallguy, the personification of established religion.

17　Avalokitesvara (*spyan-ras-gzigs*), 'He who gazes upon the world with tearful eyes', is depicted iconographically holding a crystal rosary, a white lotus, and a Wish-fulfilling Gem, in his four hands.

18　The Creative and Fulfilment Stages (*bskyed-rim dang rdzogs-rim*) are technical terms referring to the complex, formal meditative processes of generating a universal *mandala* and then attaining its consummation through realization of its 'Empty' nature.

19　Chung (rhyming with tongue) is barley, wheat, rice, or millet wine prepared by fermenting the boiled grain with the catalytic agent 'pap', saturating it with water and draining off the solution; it is a ubiquitous food, beverage, and liquor, throughout Greater Tibet.

20　The following lines would inform the initiate of the great strength and depth of Drukpa Kunley's realization – they indicate the Four Roots of his spiritual being: his Lama, Palden Drukpa Rimpoche, reincarnated as *Lha-btsun kun-dga' chos-kyi rgya-mtsho* (1432–1505); his YIDAM or personal deity, Chakrasamvara, the principal Deity of the Kahgyupas; his Dakini or female counterpart, his anima of perfect awareness, Vajra Varahi; and his Protector, The Four-Armed Mahakala.

21　The Bhutanese woman plays upon the double meaning of Drukpa – an initiate of the Drukpa Kahgyu School and a native of Bhutan.

22　The Dakini is the actuality of perfect awareness, and may be encountered by the Adept as a wrathful and apparently malignant adversary or a sublime ally who bestows the capacity for fully conscious magical activities, as a spiritual entity or an incarnate woman. Orgyen is the Land of the Dakinis.

23 Orgyen, geographically located in the Swat Valley, Pakistan, is a mythic realm of Adepts, Dakinis, and Tantric Revelation.

24 The unity of these two aspects (*shes-rab dang thabs*) of the Buddhas' Being, symbolized by the *Yab-Yum* image, creates the invincible awareness that destroys all kinds of emotional dullness and ignorance.

25 The Ten Enemies (*zhing bcu*) are vicious, obstructing forces of temptation that populate every part of the spiritual universe.

26 Samsara is the realm of transmigration and emotional confusion.

27 The Three Realms (*khams gsum*) are the sensual realm, the aesthetic realm, and the formless realm – a triple division of mundane consciousness.

28 The Jowo Temple (Rasa Tulnang) in Lhasa houses the most sacred and ancient Tibetan image of Sakyamuni Buddha in the form of Vairocana – a dowry gift to Srongtsen Gampo from the King of Nepal in the 7th century. A popular legend avers that Drukpa Kunley finally vanished into the nostril of Jowo.

29 Tsampa is roast barley flour, eaten with tea or made into dough with butter; tsampa and chung form the Tibetan's staple diet.

30 The body's substantiality dissolves into light upon the attainment of Buddhahood beyond the Fourth Degree of Meditation (the 4th *dhyana*).

Chapter Two (pages 53-73)

1 Samye, south of Lhasa, was Tibet's first monastery, designed as a *mandala* by the Great Guru Padma Sambhava and financed by King Trisong Detsen in 749 AD.

2 The *mDo-sde-mchod-pa* is an annual Nyingma celebration of the Sutras.

3 The rite of Vow Restoration (*bskyang-bso*) restores the SAMAYA of union with the Three Roots, and renews the vows sworn by demons subjugated by Padma Sambhava to serve the initiate who invokes them. The following liturgy is a parody.

4 This ritual exorcism (*mdos-rgyag*) lures the spirit to be exorcized within an effigy of the afflicted party, and then caught within the spirit-trap it is destroyed when the effigy is broken. See Chapter 4.

5 This rite, which repels and dissolves (*bzdog-pa*) demons, malignant spirits, and evil forces, is in two parts; the higher part removes obstacles from the Path of the Adept in his progress towards Buddhahood, and the lower part coerces magical and mundane powers to achieve success for the Adept.

6 This communal feast (*tshogs-'khor*, *Ganacakra*) propitiates the elements of the *mandala*, particularly the Protectors, so that they

perform the functions dictated by the Adept. Failure to sustain these regular propitiatory rites results in a wild rampage of unleashed Protectors.

7 The Guardian Protectors destroy the renegade entities of the ten spheres of the spiritual universe, inducting them into their retinues, eliminating their independent existence.

8 Curd, milk, and butter, and molasses, honey and sugar.

9 Gomchens (*sgom-chen*) are ascetics and hermits devoted to long periods of meditation incarcerated in caves or sealed rooms, or, in this case, living in isolated communities served by nuns.

10 Perhaps to conceal the secrets of the dungeons, it was customary for warlords to massacre the labourers who built their fortresses.

11 Pollution of water and unhygienic disposal of waste incites the guardian serpents (*klu*, *naga*) of earth and water to spread disease, withhold rain, or send floods.

12 Rinpung is a fortress city south of Lhasa from which a dynasty of chieftains dominated central Tibet in the fifteenth and sixteenth centuries.

13 OM MANI PEME HUNG, the mantra of Avalokitesvara, the Protector of Tibet, is transliterated according to the colloquial pronunciation.

14 *Thugs-rje chen-po*, the eleven-headed, thousand-armed form of Avalokitesvara, is an emanation that the Buddha Amitabha projected upon finding himself confronted with the daunting task of liberating all beings, constantly, from the frustration and anxiety of Samsara.

15 Dorje Chung, Vajradhara, the Root Lama of the Kahgyu Tradition, and *Adi-Buddha*, is incarnate as Palden Drukpa Rimpoche.

16 Nirvana, in this context, means release from the round of birth and death, and the cycles of mental states.

17 Drepung, near Lhasa, founded in 1414, was the largest of Tibet's monastic academies, where the majority of its 7000 monks strove to attain the Geshey Degree under rigorous discipline. This academy of the Gelukpa School was famed for its knowledge of the *Kalacakra Tantra*.

18 The moral guard (*chos-khrims-pa* or *tshul-khrims-pa*) enforced discipline in the monastic towns aided by cudgels and heavy boots.

19 Sera, an academy founded in 1417 by Khedup Je, was a zealous rival of Drepung.

20 *Mahamudra*, The Magnificent or Sublime Stance (*Chakchen*), is the mystic's non-dual state of no-mind synonymous with Buddhahood; initially verbalized by Saraha, it is the ultimate aim of all practitioners of the Tantras. Drukpa Kunley exemplifies *Mahamudra* realization.

21 Tsongkhapa (1357-1419), born in Amdo, known as Amdo Big-Nose, possessed an immense and towering intellect, and is, therefore, described as an incarnation of Manjusri, the Bodhisattva of Intelligence; instigating moral reform within the Kadampa School, he paved the way for the Gelukpa theocracy of the Dalai Lamas of Lhasa.

22   Manjusri, Protector of the Mind, Bodhisattva of Intelligence, holds the sword that cuts through ignorance, and the Book of Transcendent Wisdom resting on a blue lotus.

23   Ramoche houses the image of Sakyamuni given as dowry to King Srongtsen Gampo by the Emperor of China in the 7th century; it was also the sanctuary of a powerful oracle. Tsongkhapa lived permanently outside Lhasa at Galden.

24   The rGyal-'gong demon is a demonic entity preying upon the weak, young, and infirm, inducing nervous disease and insanity.

25   The Tibetan word used here is *Dorje* (*Vajra*), which is the name of the three, four, or nine-pronged ritual instrument symbolizing the diamond-like awareness and the adamantine strength of Emptiness; originally, it was the symbol of Indra's (or Jove's) Thunderbolt. Esoterically, and euphemistically, the *Dorje* is the penis as the lotus is the vagina.

26   Machik Palden Lhamo, Protectress of Lhasa, rides a mule and holds a flaming sword and a skull cup.

27   Atisha, Dipankara Sri Jnana (980-1042), was invited to Tibet from Vikramasila in Bengal, and founded the Kadampa School that Tsongkapa was to reform and glorify.

28   The blue, ten-thousand-petalled lotus, the Utpala Lotus, is Manjusri's symbol.

29   A thread, knotted and blessed by a Lama and worn around the neck by devotees, is a protective talisman and source of spiritual power.

Chapter Three (pages 74-86)

1   The Taklung Monastery, north-east of Lhasa, was founded by Taklung Thangpa, a disciple of Phakmotrupa in 1178, and became the seat of the Taklung Kahgyu School.

2   'Sage' is a rendering of Tokden (*rtogs-ldan*), a Gomchen who has gained realization of the essentially 'Empty' nature of mind.

3   A Tulku (*sprul-sku*) is a Buddha Lama incarnate in successive lives to rule, teach, and inspire his disciples in his particular monastery.

4   The consort (*gsang-yum* or *mudra*) is a Dakini partner in Third Initiation Rites and the means whereby an incarnation may enter the world.

5   The Karmapas are Tulkus of Dusum Khyenpo, founder of the largest of the Kahgyu Schools, the Karma Kahgyu. Their principal monastery is at Tsurphu. The black hat referred to here is probably an initiatory hat, and not the famous Black Hat woven of Dakini Hair and empowering the wearer to flight.

6   The hook and noose are standard appurtenances of spiritual entities intent upon capturing and binding the minds of the unwary and passionate.

7   Ogmin, 'Not Least', is the highest of the sensual realms, where the body is etherialized.

8 See Chapter 1, note 5.

9 The principal protector of the Karma Kahgyu School is Ber-nag, Black Cloak.

10 Sakya Panchen, (*Kun-dga' rgyal-mtshan*), the third ecclesiastical hierarch of the Sakya School, an emanation of Manjusri, converted the Mongol Emperor Kublai Khan, and achieved political hegemony for the Sakyas over Tibet; he was also responsible for the creation of the Uigur alphabet. The School's seat was founded in the city of Sakya (Yellow Earth) by Konchok Gyalpo, a disciple of Atisha, in 1071, and it quickly gained a reputation for exact scholarship.

11 Jampa (*byams-pa*, Maitreya), is the immanent Buddha of Loving Kindness, depicted iconographically sitting western style in a chair. The Rite of Mourning (*dgongs-rdzogs*) implores the Tulku to return to Samsara for the sake of all beings.

12 Bodhisattvas rest in Galden (*Tushita*) before returning as Tulkus to Samsara to fulfil their vow of selfless service.

13 Vajrasattva, as the principal of the mandala, possesses the five aspects of ultimate awareness (*Ye-shes, jnana*): its mirror-like quality, its sameness in every form, its clarity of discrimination, its miraculous efficiency, and its absolute reality.

14 The Kon or 'Kon are an ancient Clan of Western Tibet.

15 The *Lan-tsha* (*rajna*) script is a decorative script used by Northern Buddhists since the 7th century.

16 Jomo Lhari is a mountain on the border of Tibet and Bhutan.

17 A great and ancient kingdom south of the Ganges in Bihar, which was the nucleus of Ashoka's empire, and which is the Holy Land of the Buddhists.

18 The Ten Virtues, which Buddhist Kings including and succeeding Ashoka made the centre of their political law, are abstinence from killing, stealing, and sexual misconduct, supression of lying, cursing, slander, and idle talk, and rejection of malicious, covetous, or opinionated, thoughts.

Chapter Four (pages 87-102)

1 The six realms are the realms of the gods, titans, human beings, hungry ghosts, beasts and denizens of hell; all sentient life is subsumed within these classes.

2 A Stupa (*mchod-rten*), receptacle of offerings or object of worship, is a tower-like monument with a dome resting upon a graduated plinth; its geometry symbolizes various aspects of the Buddhas' enlightenment.

3 The Eight Sugata Stupas are the Stupa of Enlightenment, the Piled Lotus Stupa, the Auspicious Stupa, the Magical Stupa, the Gods Landing Place Stupa, the Stupa of Reconciliation, the Victorious Stupa, and the Nirvana Stupa; each differs in minor points of design.

4 The god and patron of the arts and crafts is Vishvakarman.

5   The Thirteen Wheels are the discs forming the tower of the Stupa, symbolizing the grades of the Bodhisattva Path and the Three Bodies of the Buddhas.

6   The Saviouress, the sublimely beautiful goddess Drolma (Arya Tara), is the personification of active compassion and effective devotion.

7   Taking refuge in the Buddha involves uncompromising renunciation and a metaphorical return to the pure potential of the womb; and insofar as the female organ represents penetrating insight (*prajna, sherab*), 'entering the *mandala* between woman's thighs' is a metaphor for consummation of the union of *Dorje* and *Padma*, Guru and Dakini, and Skilful Means and Penetrating Insight.

8   Sengdeng is the acacia tree, but here it is understood as the dense sub-tropical forest of Assam and Northern Bengal.

9   The Vinaya is the law of moral discipline: the Four Root Vows are the spiritual SAMAYA-s of the Buddhas' Body, Speech, and Mind, and the Ultimate SAMAYA, and the subsidiary vows are the practical ramifications of these vows.

10   Tashi Lhumpo, near Shigatse, was the seat of the Panchen Lamas, emanations of the Buddha Amitabha, rivals of the Dalai Lamas in political influence, and their superiors in spiritual clout.

11   The Glorious Goddess (Machik Palden Lhamo) is a popular form of the terrible Protectress Mahakali.

12   To open the mouth and show the tongue is a sign of greeting and humility.

13   After Milarepa's father died, his widowed mother suffered similarly at the hands of relatives.

14   Buddha taught that the body is a compound (*phung-po*, heap) consisting of form, feeling, conception, impulse, and consciousness.

Chapter Five (pages 103-118)

1   'White' or 'Righteous' Lineage (*dkar-brgyud*) is a synonym and virtual homonym of 'Oral' Lineage, Kahgyu (*bka'-brgyud*).

2   *Tsa-ri rdza-spyil* is south of Kongpo in Dakpo province.

3   Shar Daklha Gampo is the eastern monastery of Dwags-po Lha-rje of sGam-po (Gampopa), a principal disciple of Milarepa.

4   This monthly or seasonal observance (*smyung-gnas*) is an opportunity for laymen to renew their vows through prostration before the Great Compassionate One (*Thugs-rje chen-po*). The litany of obeisance is divided into two parts: the first part is a humble invocation of the most sacred in order to gain Buddhahood; and the second part is a tolerant acceptance of the profane in order to obtain mundane power and success; thus both relative power and ultimate realization (*siddhi*) is gained. This litany is, of course, a parody.

5   The Chenga Tulkus, hierarchs of the Drigung Kahgyupas, are reincarnations of a disciple of Phamotrupa (1110-1170) with their

seat at Thel (near Daklha Gampo) and Drigung.

6   Perhaps Lhaje Sonam Rinchen is another of Lhatsunpa's names.

7   The Eight Mundane Preoccupations are pleasure and pain, praise and blame, profit and loss, and fame and ignominy.

8   Galden was the first and principal monastery founded by Tsongkhapa, and was famed for the rigorous academic and moral discipline that gave the Gelukpa School its name. The visionary who named it saw it as a reflection of the Tushita Heaven.

9   The practitioners of the Chod Rite (*gcod-yul-pa*) are Tantric Buddhists who perform an essentially shamanistic rite in which legions of Dakinis and spirits are invoked to feed upon the flesh of the ritualist in a purificatory expiation.

10 The Noichin Apsara (*gnod-spyin ap-sa-ra*) is Lord of the Hungry Ghosts and Master of Wealth; rebirth as such is induced through a *samadhi* in which avarice is the motivating force and the object of contemplation.

11 The Threefold Commitment (*sdom-pa gsum*) is commitment to the physical and moral discipline of the Hinayana, to the Bodhisattva Vow of the Mahayana, and to the SAMAYA-s of the Vajrayana.

12 The communal feast or sacrament (*tshogs-'khor*) is a propitiation of the Buddha Protectors by offerings of all kinds, including the barley cake *torma*-s.

13 Sangye Tsenchen (1452-1507), who compiled the 'Life of Milarepa', and Kunga Zangpo (1458-1532), are revered equally with Drukpa Kunley as divinity incarnate to teach through crazy-wisdom.

14 *Heruka*-s are *Naljorpa*-s, who upon completion of the Creative and Fulfilment Stages of invocation of a particular terrific Deity become identical in power and awareness to that Deity.

15 *Cog-bu-pa*-s are nomadic people of Bhutan characterized by their small black tents.

16 *sTag-ras-pa* - 'he who wears a tiger skin'.

17 Bumthang is an ancient fortress settlement of central Bhutan situated on a plain (*thang*) shaped like a flask (*Bum*).

18 Bhutan emerged as a fixed political entity only in the nineteenth century. Mon (devoid of *Dharma*) is the Tibetan name for the cis-Himalyas from the Sherpa lands to Nagaland. Lho or Lho-nang (The South), Lho Mon (South Mon, translated herein as Bhutan), Lho Rong (the Southern Ravines), Lho Jong (the Southern Valleys) refer specifically to the area through which Drukpa Kunley wandered, which is called by the Bhutanese themselves Drukyul, the Land of the Dragon Folk.

19 Until recently in India it was customary in some areas for girls to spend nights of divine nuptials in a temple, 'that god may descend upon them'; in Greater Tibet wandering Naljorpas would teach girls the rudiments of sexual activity.

20 Peppercorns (*gyer-ma*) are worth their weight in gold where spices are a great luxury.

21 The Terton Orgyen Pema Lingpa (1445-1521) was an emanation of

the Great Guru Padma Sambhava; he was Longchen Rabjampa in a previous life, the fourth of the Five Poet-Kings, and recipient of 108 revelations of the Great Guru himself. Tertons (Treasure Finders or Enlightened Poets) are mystics and scholars of the Nyingma School able to discover and decipher relevant scriptures written in the language of the Dakinis and concealed originally by Padma Sambhava.

22   The Great Perfection or Sublime Consummation (*rdzogs-chen*) is the apogee of mystic attainment, and its practices are the fastest course to Buddhahood; the initiate is immediately introduced to the centre of the *mandala*, where, with only his SAMAYA-S as support, he stands to realize his own mind as the universal *mandala* of 'Emptiness'. The goal of *Mahamudra* is identical, but the path more gentle and the dangers less acute.

23   Mount Tise is Kailash, the lingam-shaped mountain in western Tibet considered to be the *axis mundi*, Mount Meru, by both Bud-dhist and Hindu Asia; for the Hindus it is the abode of Shiva and Parvati, and for the Buddhists it is the Paradise of Chakra-samvara.

24   Diamond Being (*Vajrasattva*) is the personification of Mirror-like Awareness; a unity of male (*Dorje*) and female (bell) forces, it is a general term for a Vajrayana Preceptor.

25   The Creative Stage of attention to form, and the Fulfilment Stage of realization of form as Emptiness, must be practised simultaneously. See Chapter 1, note 18.

Chapter Six (pages 119-136)

1   Dusol Lhamo (Dhumavati Devi), which is a form of the Protectress Palden Lhamo.

2   Winter is the dry season in Bhutan.

3   *sTod-pa si-lung 'gram og-ma.*

4   *Phag-ri sprel-mo la* is the pass connecting *Lho-brag* in Tibet with the *sPa-gro* Valley in Bhutan.

5   Demons (male and female, *bdud-po* and *bdud-mo*), in the popular mind, as in medieval Europe, are considered to be external, discrete entities; but in the higher, intentional learning of the Lamas, they are treated as projections of the vicious or passionate elements of the collective mind, alienated forces requiring integration into the whole mandala, or communal psychoses that can be cured or transformed. In the same way the Great Guru Padma Sambhava subjugated the demons of Tibet and included them within the mandala as terrific mask-like protectors and benevolent agents of the Teaching, Drukpa Kunley converted the demons of Bhutan through his fearlessness and perfect awareness.

6   Clay is stamped upon or beaten with a flailing stick to prepare it for building purposes.

7   The *bardo* is the intermediate space between death and rebirth, between one thought and the next, where one's karmic chickens come home to roost, and where it is possible to gain freedom from transmigration.

8   The lesser vows refer to the lay vows to refrain from killing, stealing, sexual misconduct, intoxicants, and lying.

9   *Dar-so-che-ba* or *dar-sar-byed-ba* (?) – to perpetuate ritual observances and offerings to a minor guardian protector.

10 *Pha-jo'i sras gsang-gdag gar-ston* (1183-1251) was the principal disciple of Palden Drukpa Rimpoche; he led a migration of Drukpa Kahgyupas to Bhutan and established the Drukpa Dharma there. Reborn as Drukpa Kunley's son *Ngag-dbang bstan-'dzin* (1520-90), whose Guru was the abbot *Ngag-gi dbang-phyug* (1517-54) and who founded the Thimpu *rTa-mgo* Hermitage, his title, *Pha-jo*, passed to *Ngag-dbang bstan-'dzin*'s son, *Mi-pham tshe-dbang bstan-'dzin* (*Pha-jo rta-mgrin rgyal-mtshan*, 1574-1643). Of *Mi-phan*'s sons, *sGrub-thob sbyin-pa rgyal-mtshan* had no offspring, and *rGyal-sras bstan-'dzin rab-rgyas* produced only a daughter, known as *lCam kun-legs*, who became the first of the *rTa-mgo bLa-ma* incarnations.

11 *gNam-'phar 'bebs-chad* literally means 'Holding aloft, bringing down, cessation', in the manner of monks lifting one cymbal high in the air and letting it fall forcefully to let the sound cease suddenly.

12 The Chung Tung is the vast deserted plateau country of north western Tibet, which the Chinese claim to have partially irrigated and cultivated.

13 *Chu-bdud mtsho-sman-ma.*

14 The refuge (*skyabs-'gro*) is the initial vow of commitment to the Buddha, his Path, and his Brotherhood.

15 The seed syllable AH is the sound of Emptiness, the all-pervasive unborn essence.

16 The Khyi-med (No-dog) Temple (or Khyi-'bur, as it has been known) is the chief seat of Drukpa Kunley in Bhutan.

Chapter Seven (pages 137-156)

1   It is noteworthy that Kunley never eats meat without returning the life of the slaughtered animal.

2   This is a species of wild yak ('*brong-gim-tshe*).

3   To lay men and women the Lama teaches worldly wisdom laced with basic instruction in sexual behaviour. Such oral transmission preceded the classroom as the means of educating the young in every sphere; the 'dirty' joke is often the first source of a child's information about sex even in our society.

4   The Three Vehicles are the *Hinayana*, *Mahayana*, and *Vajrayana*. The first teaches those who can easily suppress passion; the second teaches those who can transform passion into positive energies; and the third teaches those who can utilize passion for the benefit of others.

5 Shar Kunzangling in the Wongdu district was the seat of Longchen
   Rabjampa during his period of self-exile from Tibet in the 14th
   century.

6 The distilled essence of chung is a clear and very potent spirit called
   arak or *rakshi*.

7 Although Gautama Buddha's original thesis of *anatman* implies that
   man has no substantial 'soul', the utilitarian doctrine of metempsy-
   chosis postulates a conglomeration of genetic propensities inherent
   in a transmigrating principle of consciousness, which, in common
   belief, is virtually a substantial and eternal verity.

8 The Pure Land of Delight (*bde-ba-can*, *Sukhavati*) is Amitabha's
   Western Paradise of which the euphonic corollary is the seed-syllable
   HRI.

9 The Sakya Lama Thimbe Rabjang went to Bhutan in 1152 and
   established several Sakya monasteries there.

10 Punakha monastic fort was built on this spot as the headquarters of
   the Drukpa conquerer Ngawong Namgyal (1594–1651) after his
   great military victory at Kabang in 1636 over the combined forces of
   the Great Fifth Dalai Lama and the Mongol Gushri Khan; the
   weapons captured in this battle were stashed in the Punakha fort and
   can still be seen.

11 Maphamyu, Indestructible Turquoise, is the Tibetan name of Lake
   Manasarovar near Mount Kailash; it is the source of the Brahma-
   putra. The fish of this lake, like most fish in Tibet, were sacrosanct.

12 The Four Joys, or grades of ecstasy, are joy, supreme joy, beyond
   joy and ultimate spontaneous joy, each associated with one of the
   four principal focal points of psychic energy (gut, heart, throat, and
   fontanelle).

13 The Fountain of Truth (*chos-'byung*), the Origin of Dharma, is
   penetrating insight into the nature of the metamorphosing phan-
   tasmagoria of illusion as Emptiness, which in the Mahayana is
   personified as the Goddess Mahaprajnaparamitama; in the Tantras,
   non-dual, ultimate awareness of Empty illusion is the Dakini with
   whom the Guru unites in sublime delight; in the sexual analogy, the
   Fountain of Truth is the vagina (*bhaga*); to play in the Fountain of
   Truth is to meditate. In general, danger lies in believing that limited
   insight into one particular level of meaning endows that meaning
   with incontravertible, exclusive significance.

14 See Chapter 6, note 16.

15 Of the many hidden valleys discovered by the Great Guru Padma
   Sambhava that possess secret entrances to his Paradise, *sBas-yul
   Padma Tsal* (*Padma bkod*) on the Tibet–Assam border is of greatest
   renown.

16 The Dragon Planet (*Rahu*) is the mythological planet and demon
   that is said to chase the moon and consume it temporarily at the time
   of eclipse.

17 Chakdar (*Phyag-mda'*) is the area of To where Drukpa Kunley's
   arrow fell.

Chapter Eight (pages 157-173)

1 The five poisons of the psyche are lust, hatred, pride, jealousy, and sloth.

2 This most significant of public rites (*bka'-dbang*) usually begins with a sermon devoted to the exposition of moral and mental disciplines, and climaxes in an Empowerment, Consecration, and Initiation into the mandala of a particular Deity.

3 The flask (*bum-pa*) of ambrosia is filled with the consecrated liquid that confers the empowerment of the Deity as the initiate drinks it.

4 The Tibetan people make a customary token libation of whatever food or drink they consume (*phud-gtor*).

5 The custom of self-immolation of widows in India was outlawed under the British Raj, and in Nepal it is unthinkable nowadays.

6 Drukpa Kunley's first son was known by the name of the field into which his father had thrown him (Chapter 4). The monastery that Zhingkyong Drukda founded is in the valley of mTshur-phu in the area of sTod-yul.

7. At the *parinirvana* of a Buddha, flesh and blood dissolve into light which vanishes into the appropriate paradise, while the essence of his being precipitates as small silvery balls (*ring-bsrel*). Drukpa Kunley preferred to leave his bones behind him in the form of various Buddha images.

8 Shabdung (*Zhabs-drung*) Rimpoche is another name of Ngawong Namgyal. See Chapter 7, note 10.

APPENDIX 1
Map of Tibet and Bhutan

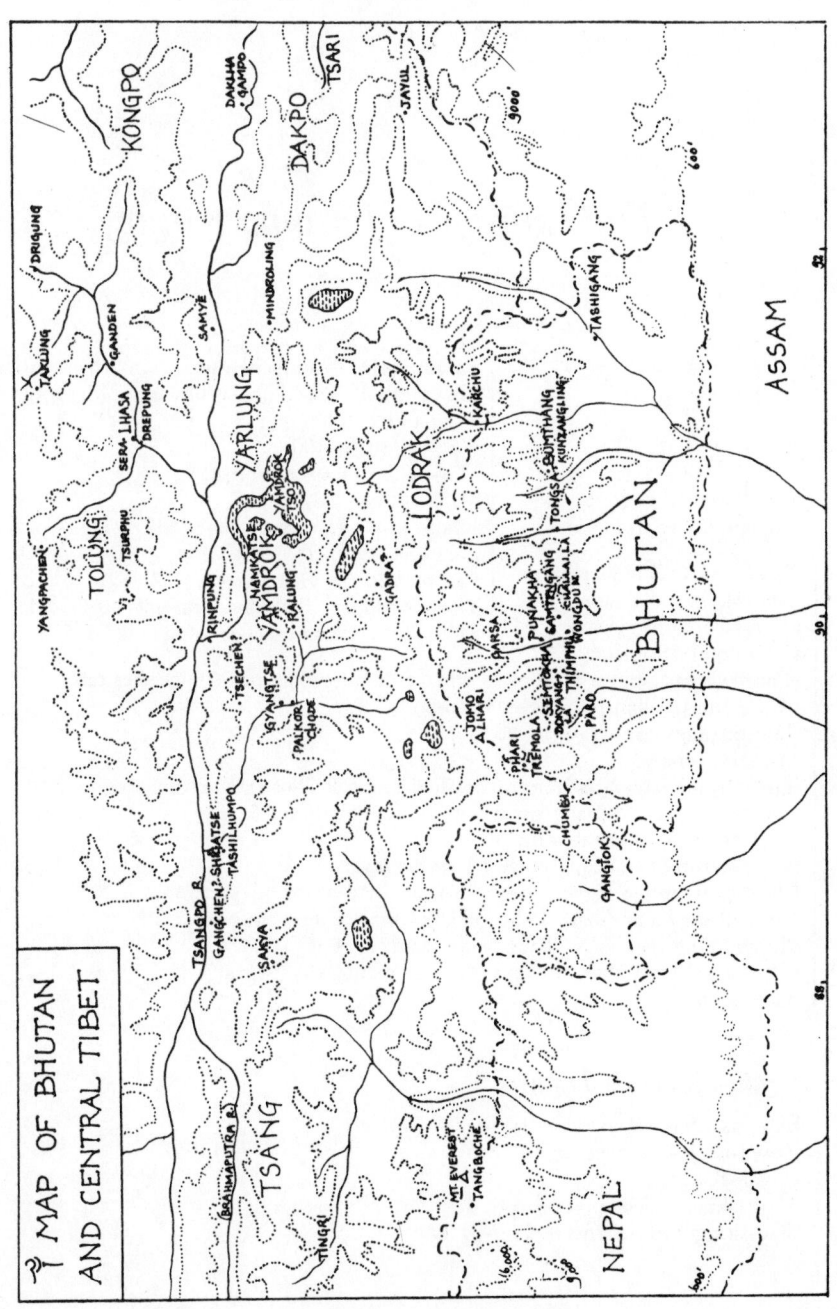

The Lineage of Drukpa Kunley

Saraha, mDa'-bsnun chen-po (*c.* 8th-9th centuries)
Shavaripa, Ri-khrod dbang-phyug (*c.* 9th century)
Tilopa (988-1069)
Naropa (1016-1100)
Mar-pa the Translator (1012-97)
Mi-la-ras-pa (1052-1136)
sGam-po-pa, Dwags-po lha-rje (1079-1153)
Phag-mo-gru-pa (1110-70)
Pad-ma rdo-rje, gLing ras-pa (1128-89)
Ye-shes rdo-rje, dPal-ldan 'brug-pa (1161-1211)
Pha-jo'i sras gsang-bdag gar-ston (1183-1251)

*The blood lineage of
Tsangpa Gyaru*

Gya'i rus-can Zur-po tsha-pe
m. Ma-bza' dar-skyid &
gCen Lha-'bum-gyi sras
sLob-dpon/dBon-stag
sPos-skya-pa chen-po Seng-ge rin-chen & rDo-rje gling-pa Seng-ge shes-rab
bCu-gsum-pa chen-po Seng-ge rgyal-po
'Jam-dbyangs kun-dga' seng-ge
bLo-gros seng-ge
'Jam-dbyangs sprul-pa Nam-mkha' dpal-bzang & Chos-rje Shes-rab seng-ge
rDo-rje rgyal-po & gSang-sprul Nam-mkha' dpal-bzang &
   sPyan-sprul Shes-rab seng-ge
Nang-so Rin-chen bzang-po *m.* dGon-mo skyid
Chos-rje Kun-dga' legs-pa (1455-1570) *m.* dPal-bzang bu-'khrid-mo
Ngag-dbang bstan-'dzin (1520-1590) & Zhing-skyong 'brug-sgra
Pha-jo'i yang-srid Tshe-dbang bstan-'dzin (1574-1643)
rGyal-sras bStan-'dzin rab-rgyas & Grub-mchog sByin-rgyal
lCam Kun-legs

Drukpa Kunley's Teachers

bLa-ma gNas-rnying chos-rje
Zhwa-lu rJe-mkhyen rab-pa
rGyal-dbang rje
rTogs-ldan Lha-btsun chen-po
dGe-slong bSod-rnams mchog-pa

MORE TITLES ON TIBET
FROM PILGRIMS PUBLISHING

www.pilgrimsbooks.com

PILGRIMS BOOK HOUSE
B. 27/98 A-8 Nawab Ganj Road, Durga Kund Varanasi 221010
Tel. 91-542-2314060 Fax. 91-542-2312456
E-mail: pilgrimsbooks@sify.com

PILGRIMS BOOK HOUSE (New Delhi)
2391, Tilak Street, Chuna Mandi
Paharganj, New Delhi 110055
Tel: (91-11) 23584015, 23584839 Fax: 23584019
E-mail: pilgrimsinde@gmail.com

PILGRIMS BOOK HOUSE (Kathmandu)
P O Box 3872, Thamel, Kathmandu, Nepal
Tel: 977-1-4700942, Off: 977-1-4700919,
Fax: 977-1-4700943
E-mail: pilgrims@wlink.com.np